Apache Cassandra Essentials

Create your own massively scalable Cassandra
database with highly responsive database queries

Nitin Padalia

BIRMINGHAM - MUMBAI

Apache Cassandra Essentials

First published: November 2015

Production reference: 1161115

Published by Packt Publishing Ltd.
Livery Place
35 Livery Street
Birmingham B3 2PB, UK.

ISBN 978-1-78398-910-2

www.packtpub.com

Credits

Author
Nitin Padalia

Reviewers
Ranjeet Kumar Jha
Sonal Raj
Chaoran Yu

Commissioning Editor
Akram Hussain

Acquisition Editor
Meeta Rajani

Content Development Editor
Aparna Mitra

Technical Editor
Rohan Uttam Gosavi

Copy Editor
Pranjali Chury

Project Coordinator
Mary Alex

Proofreader
Safis Editing

Indexer
Mariammal Chettiyar

Graphics
Disha Haria

Production Coordinator
Nilesh Mohite

Cover Work
Nilesh Mohite

About the Author

Nitin Padalia is the technical leader at Aricent Group, where he is involved in building highly scalable distributed applications in the field of telecommunications. From the beginning of his career, he has been working in the field of telecommunications and has worked on protocols such as SMPP, RTP, SIP, and VOIP. Since the beginning of his career, he has worked on the development of applications that can scale infinitely with highest performance possible. He has experience of developing applications for bare metal hardware, virtualized environments, and cloud-based applications using various languages and technologies.

I would like to thank all the reviewers of this book; their comments helped me to present data effectively.

Meeta Rajani, for setting things up and providing input during the initial phase of the book.

Anish Sukumaran, for helping me through his comments and input till the completion of this book.

Chaoran Yu, for good suggestions regarding presenting data and examples in a way that could be more helpful from the readers' perspective.

Ranjit, for his input throughout the book.

I also would like to thank my family—my mother, father, wife, and kids—for letting me take some time out to write this book.

About the Reviewers

Ranjeet Kumar Jha has over 12 years (three years in the big data field) of experience in various phases of the project life cycle, including the development and design phases. He has also been part of production support for Java/JEE and big data-based applications. He is a certified enterprise architect, that is, Oracle Certified Master Enterprise Java JEE Architect, and has worked for over six years as an architect in Java JEE technologies (over three years in the big data field). He has worked in various domains such as finance, insurance, e-commerce, digital media, CMS, security, and online advertisements.

He has worked as a programmer, designer, mentor, and architect on all types of projects related to Java, especially JEE and big data. He is the reviewer of the book *Real-time Analytics with Storm and Cassandra*.

To find out more about him, visit his LinkedIn profile at `https://www.linkedin.com/in/jharanjeet`.

I would like to thank my family—my wife, Anila Jha, and two kids, Anushka Jha and Tanisha Jha, for their constant support, encouragement, and patience. Without you, I wouldn't have achieved so much! Love you all immensely.

Sonal Raj is a hacker, Pythonista, big data believer, and a technology dreamer. He has a passion for design and is an artist at heart. He blogs about technology, design, and gadgets at `http://www.sonalraj.com/`. When not working on projects, he can be found travelling, stargazing, or reading.

He has pursued engineering in computer science and holds a master's degree in IT. He loves to work on community projects. He has been a research fellow at IISc and has taken up projects on graph computations using Neo4j, Storm, and NoSQL databases. He has been a speaker at PyCon India and local meetups and has also published articles and research papers in leading magazines and international journals. He has contributed to several open source projects.

He is the author of *Neo4j High Performance, Packt Publishing*, and has reviewed titles on technologies such as Storm and Neo4j

I am grateful to the author for patiently listening to my critiques. I'd like to thank the open source community for keeping their passions alive and contributing to such remarkable projects. A special thank you to my parents, without whom I never would have grown to love learning as much as I do.

Chaoran Yu obtained his bachelor's degree with high honors from UC Berkeley Department of Electrical Engineering and Computer Science in May 2014. He has been a software developer with the data analytics team of Ericsson MediaFirst, a leading IPTV solution, since then. The technologies that he has worked on include Apache Cassandra, Spark, and the Microsoft .NET framework. He organized service and client logging and performance data and wrote code to store them in Cassandra, which he then processed with Spark jobs to generate real-time reports for TV operators. His passion for open source technologies, especially for distributed and scalable systems, makes him an avid learner in this ever-changing technology landscape.

www.PacktPub.com

Support files, eBooks, discount offers, and more

For support files and downloads related to your book, please visit www.PacktPub.com.

Did you know that Packt offers eBook versions of every book published, with PDF and ePub files available? You can upgrade to the eBook version at www.PacktPub.com and as a print book customer, you are entitled to a discount on the eBook copy. Get in touch with us at service@packtpub.com for more details.

At www.PacktPub.com, you can also read a collection of free technical articles, sign up for a range of free newsletters and receive exclusive discounts and offers on Packt books and eBooks.

https://www2.packtpub.com/books/subscription/packtlib

Do you need instant solutions to your IT questions? PacktLib is Packt's online digital book library. Here, you can search, access, and read Packt's entire library of books.

Why subscribe?

- Fully searchable across every book published by Packt
- Copy and paste, print, and bookmark content
- On demand and accessible via a web browser

Free access for Packt account holders

If you have an account with Packt at www.PacktPub.com, you can use this to access PacktLib today and view 9 entirely free books. Simply use your login credentials for immediate access.

Table of Contents

Preface

Traditional database management systems sometimes become the bottleneck of being highly available, scalable, and ultra responsive for modern day applications, as they are not able to satisfy the storage and retrieval needs of modern applications with all these attributes. Apache Cassandra being a highly available, massively scalable, NoSQL, query-driven database helps our applications to achieve these modern day must have attributes. Apache Cassandra's core features include handling of large data with the flexibility of configuring responsiveness, scalability, and high availability at the same time to suit our requirements.

In this book, I've provided step-by-step information starting from the basic installation to the advanced installation options and database design techniques. It gives all the information that you will need to design a well-distributed and high performance database. This book focuses on explaining core concepts with simple and easy-to-understand examples. I've also incorporated some code examples with this book. You can use these examples while working on your day-to-day tasks with Cassandra.

What this book covers

Chapter 1, *Getting Your Cassandra Cluster Ready*, gives an introduction to Cassandra and helps you to set up your cluster. It also introduces you to the various configuration options available to set up your cluster, which can be referred to while fine tuning the cluster.

Chapter 2, *An Architectural Overview*, helps you to understand the internal architecture of a Cassandra cluster. It details various strategies used by Cassandra to distribute data among various nodes in the cluster. It describes how Cassandra becomes highly available by employing various replication strategies. It also clarifies various replication and data distribution strategies.

Chapter 3, Creating Database and Schema, details the concepts used by Cassandra. We'll learn to use CQL (Cassandra Query Language), which is used by Cassandra clients to describe data models, to create our databases and tables. Also, we'll discuss various techniques provided by Cassandra that can be used based on our storage and data retrieval requirements.

Chapter 4, Read and Write – Behind the Scenes, has been written keeping in mind how the reader can understand core concepts of a system. We'll discuss the operations that Cassandra performs for every read and write query along with all the data structures and caches it uses. We'll also discuss what configuration options it provides to configure the trade-off between consistency and latency. In the later parts of this chapter, we'll see how we can trace a Cassandra read/write query to debug performance issues for our read/write queries.

Chapter 5, Writing Your Cassandra Client, provides some code samples to set up your cluster, learn the core concepts of Cassandra, and create your database and schema. Now comes the time to know how our application will connect to the Cassandra cluster and perform a read/write operation.

Chapter 6, Monitoring and Tuning a Cassandra Cluster, covers various tools that can be used to monitor your Cassandra cluster. After you set up your application and cluster, it is necessary to know how to monitor your Cassandra cluster in order to run it successfully consistently. We'll also discuss various tuning parameters that are used to fine-tune Cassandra with regards to our hardware or networking environments.

Chapter 7, Backup and Restore, talks about Cassandra being highly available with no single point of failure. Sometimes there could be a scenario when we would need to restore data from an old snapshot; for example; suppose some buggy client corrupted our data and we want to recover from last day's snapshot. For situations like this, Cassandra has an option to take a backup of data and use various restore techniques. You'll learn about these techniques in this chapter.

What you need for this book

In this book, we'll set up a Cassandra cluster. Cassandra server's latest code can be downloaded from `http://cassandra.apache.org/download/`. We refer to the Cassandra Server version more than or equal to 2.x in our examples; this version requires Java version more than or equal to 1.7 and Python version more than or equal to 2.6. Python is required to run the CQL client **cqlsh** provided by Cassandra. In later chapters, we use the **Datastax** Java driver as the Cassandra client; for example, the Cassandra Java driver by Datastax can be downloaded from `https://github.com/datastax/java-driver`. We will use the driver version 2.1.2 in our examples. Other than that, if you set up a cluster for your development environment, then your development machine should have at least 4 GB of RAM and at least a dual core CPU. While working with a Java client, we expect you to have a basic knowledge of Java. While working on a Cassandra client, use any IDE; for example, Eclipse (`https://eclipse.org/`), for building. I've provided dependencies according to the **Maven** (`https://maven.apache.org/`) and **Gradle** (`https://gradle.org/`) frameworks.

Who this book is for

This book is written keeping in mind developers at both beginner and intermediate level. It also includes topics on maintenance and fine tuning Cassandra also debugging your queries so that you can get the best out of it. This book is useful for all those who are working with huge datasets and since traditional relational databases are not able to satisfy their needs of high performance, availability and scalability, so they want to learn Cassandra. However, it's not required for them to be aware of traditional relational concepts. In fact, not knowing relational model at all might help in some cases because when you are designing your database, you won't be thinking about it from the traditional relational database perspective.

Conventions

In this book, you will find a number of styles of text that distinguish between different kinds of information. Here are some examples of these styles, and an explanation of their meaning.

Code words in text, database table names, folder names, filenames, file extensions, pathnames, dummy URLs, user input, and Twitter handles are shown as follows: "Apache provides source as well as binary `tarballs` and `Debian` packages."

A block of code is set as follows:

```
$ sudomkdir -p /var/log/Cassandra
$ sudochown -R `whoami` /var/log/Cassandra
$ sudomkdir -p /var/lib/Cassandra
$ sudochown -R `whoami` /var/lib/cassandra
```

Any command-line input or output is written as follows:

```
$ java -version
java version "1.7.0_45"
```

New terms and **important words** are shown in bold. Words that you see on the screen, in menus or dialog boxes for example, appear in the text like this: "OrderPreservingPartitioner is similar to above with same challenges and additional limitation that it assumes that keys are **UTF8** strings".

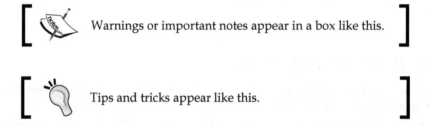

Warnings or important notes appear in a box like this.

Tips and tricks appear like this.

Reader feedback

Feedback from our readers is always welcome. Let us know what you think about this book—what you liked or may have disliked. Reader feedback is important for us to develop titles that you really get the most out of.

To send us general feedback, simply send an e-mail to feedback@packtpub.com, and mention the book title via the subject of your message.

Customer support

Now that you are the proud owner of a Packt book, we have a number of things to help you to get the most from your purchase.

Downloading the example code

Errata

Although we have taken every care to ensure the accuracy of our content, mistakes do happen. If you find a mistake in one of our books—maybe a mistake in the text or the code—we would be grateful if you would report this to us. By doing so, you can save other readers from frustration and help us improve subsequent versions of this book. If you find any errata, please report them by visiting `http://www.packtpub.com/submit-errata`, selecting your book, clicking on the **errata submission form** link, and entering the details of your errata. Once your errata are verified, your submission will be accepted and the errata will be uploaded on our website, or added to any list of existing errata, under the Errata section of that title. Any existing errata can be viewed by selecting your title from `http://www.packtpub.com/support`.

Piracy

Piracy of copyright material on the Internet is an ongoing problem across all media. At Packt, we take the protection of our copyright and licenses very seriously. If you come across any illegal copies of our works, in any form, on the Internet, please provide us with the location address or website name immediately so that we can pursue a remedy.

Please contact us at `copyright@packtpub.com` with a link to the suspected pirated material.

We appreciate your help in protecting our authors, and our ability to bring you valuable content.

Questions

You can contact us at `questions@packtpub.com` if you are having a problem with any aspect of the book, and we will do our best to address it.

1
Getting Your Cassandra Cluster Ready

In this chapter, you'll learn how to set up and run our own Cassandra cluster. We'll look at the prerequisites that need to be considered before setting up a Cassandra cluster. We'll also see a Cassandra installation layout, so that we can easily locate different configuration files, tools, and utilities later on. We will discuss key configuration options that are required for cluster deployment. Then, we'll run our cluster and use Cassandra tools to verify our cluster status, some stats, and its version.

Installation

Apache provides source as well as binary `tarballs` and `Debian` packages. However, third-party vendors, such as Datastax, provide MSI installer, Linux RPM, Debian packages, and UNIX and Mac OS X binary in the form of community edition, which is a free packaged distribution of Apache Cassandra by **Datastax**. Here, we'll cover installation using binary tarball and source tarball packages.

Prerequisites

The following are the prerequisites for installing Cassandra:

- **Hardware requirements**: Cassandra employs various caching techniques to enable ultra-fast read operations; hence more memory enables Cassandra to cache more data hence more memory would lead to better performance. Minimum 4GB memory is recommended for development environments and minimum 8GB memory for production environments. If our data set is bigger we should consider upgrading memory used by Cassandra. We'll discuss more about tuning Cassandra memory in later chapters. Similar to memory, more number of CPUs helps Cassandra to perform better as Cassandra performs its task concurrently. For bare-metal hardware, 8-core servers are recommended and for virtualized machines it's recommended that CPU cycles allocated to machines could grow on demand, for example some vendors like Rackspace and Amazon use CPU bursting. For development environments you could use single disk machine, however for production machines ideally there should be at least two disks. One disk is used for commitlog and other for storing data files called SSTables, so that I/O contention doesn't happen for both these operations. The `commitlog` file is used by Cassandra to make write requests durable. Every write request is first written to this file in append only mode and an in memory representation of column family called `memtable`.

- **Java**: Cassandra can run on Oracle/Sun JVM, OpenJDK, and IBM JVM. The current stable version of Cassandra requires Java 7 or later version. Set your `JAVA_HOME` environment variable to the correct version of Java if you are using multiple Java versions on your machine.

- **Python**: The current version of Cassandra requires Python 2.6 or above. Cassandra tools, such as `cqlsh`, are based on Python.

- **Firewall configurations**: Since we are setting up a cluster, let's see which ports are used by Cassandra on various interfaces. If the firewall blocks these ports because we fail to configure them, then our cluster won't function properly. For example, if the internode communication port is being blocked, then nodes will not be able to join the cluster.

  Lets have a look at the following table

Port/ Protocol	Configuration file	Configuration name	Firewall setting	Description
`7000/ tcp`	`cassandra.yaml`	`storage_ port`	Open among nodes in the cluster	It acts as an internode communication port in a Cassandra cluster.

Port/ Protocol	Configuration file	Configuration name	Firewall setting	Description
7001/ tcp	cassandra.yaml	ssl_ storage_ port	Open among nodes in the cluster	It is a SSL port for encrypted communication among cluster nodes.
9042/ tcp	cassandra.yaml	native_ transport_ port	Between the Cassandra client and the cluster	Cassandra clients, for example cqlsh, or clients using the JAVA driver use this port to communicate with the Cassandra server.
9160/ tcp	cassandra.yaml	rpc_port	The Thrift client and the Cassandra cluster	Thrift uses this port for client connections.
7199/ tcp	cassandra-env. sh	JMX_PORT	Between the JMX console and the Cassandra cluster	It acts as an JMX console port for monitoring the Cassandra server.

- Clock syncronization: Since Cassandra depends heavily on timestamps for data consistency purposes, all nodes of our cluster should be time synchronized. Ensure that we verify this. One of the methods we can use for time synchronization is configuring NTP on each node. **NTP (Network Time Protocol)** is widely used protocol for clock synchronization of computers over a network.

Compiling Cassandra from source and installing

The following method of installation is less used. One of the cases when we might use this method is if we're doing some optimization work on Cassandra. We'll need JDK 1.7, ANT 1.8, or later versions to compile the Cassandra code. Optionally, we can directly clone from the Cassandra Git repository or we can use the source tarball. Git client 1.7 will be required for cloning git repo.

To obtain the latest source code from Git, use the following command:

```
$ git clone http://git://git-wip-us.apache.org/repos/asf/cassandra.git
Cassandra
```

For a specific branch, use the following command:

```
$ git clone -b cassandra-<version> http://git://git-wip-us.apache.org/
repos/asf/cassandra.git
```

Use this command for version 1.2:

```
$ git clone -b cassandra-2.1.2 http://git://git-wip-us.apache.org/repos/
asf/cassandra.git
```

Then, use the `ant` command to build the code:

```
$ ant
```

Alternatively, if a proxy is needed to connect to the Internet, use the `autoproxy` flag:

```
$ ant –autoproxy
```

or

```
$ export ANT_OPTS="-Dhttp.proxyHost=<your-proxy-host> -Dhttp.
proxyPort=<your-proxy-port>"
```

Installation from a precompiled binary

Download a binary tarball from the Apache website; open it using the following command. Here, we will extract it in the /opt directory:

```
$ tar xzf apache-cassandra-<Version>.bin.tar.gz -C /opt
```

Consider the following example:

```
$ tar xzf apache-cassandra-2.1.2.bin.tar.gz -C /opt
```

Optionally, you can create a soft link as a best practice, which will help in scenarios where you need to change the installation location:

```
$ ln –s apache-cassandra-2.1.2 cassandra
```

The Cassandra installation layout may be different based on your type of installation. If you're installing using Debian or an RPM package, then the installation creates the required directories and applies the required permissions.

In older versions of Cassandra, you might need to create Cassandra log and data directories before running; by default, they are pointed to /var/lib/cassandra and /var/log/Cassandra. Running Cassandra will fail if the user running Cassandra doesn't have permissions for these paths. You can create and set permissions as shown here:

```
$ sudo mkdir -p /var/log/Cassandra
```

```
$ sudo chown -R `whoami` /var/log/Cassandra
$ sudo mkdir -p /var/lib/Cassandra
$ sudo chown -R `whoami` /var/lib/cassandra
```

The installation layout

The tarball installation layout is different from RPM or Debian packages. Let's see how they differ.

The directory layout in tarball installations

The following table shows the list of directories and their description:

Directory	Description
bin	This directory contains the startup scripts to launch the Cassandra server, the cqlsh prompt, and utility tools such as nodetool.
conf	This directory is the home of configuration files, including cassandra.yaml.
lib	This directory is Cassandra's Java dependency folder.
pylib	This directory contains Python libraries for cqlsh.
tools	Stress testing tools like cassandra-stress and other tools for example, sstable2json: which could be used to convert SSTables to JSON for debugging purposes. An SSTable or Sorted String Table is an immutable data file in disk, created for each Column Family. There could be zero or more SSTable per Column Family in every node of Cassandra cluster.
data	The Cassandra data directory will be created as soon as you start populating your Cassandra server. Its location is configured using the data_file_directories in the cassandra.yaml option.
logs	This is the default log directory. In older versions, it was /var/log/Cassandra.

The directory layout in package-based installation

The following table describes the installation layout if you use RPM or Debian packages:

Directory	Description
/var/lib/cassandra	This is the data directory.
/var/log/cassandra/	This is the log directory.
/var/run/Cassandra	This is the runtime file location, for example, the PID file.
/usr/share/Cassandra	This is the home of the include file cassandra-in.sh, which is used to set environment variables, such as CASSANDRA_HOME, CLASSPATH, and so on for Cassandra.
/usr/share/cassandra/lib	This is Cassandra's Java dependency folder; JAR files are placed here.
/usr/bin	This is the home of tools and utilities such as cqlsh, nodetool, and cassandra-stress.
/etc/cassandra	This is the home of the configuration.
/etc/init.d/	This contains the Cassandra startup scripts.
/etc/security/limits.d/	This is the file defining Cassandra user limits.

Configuration files

Now, let's look at some key configuration files and the options that we can configure in them:

cassandra.yaml

The configuration files are as follows:

- Cluster configurations

    cluster_name: This is the identification string for a logical cluster. All nodes in a cluster must have the same value for this configuration.

    Default value: The default value is Test Cluster.

`listen_address`: The Cassandra node will bind to this address. The other nodes in the cluster can communicate with this node if it is set correctly; leaving it to default will cause a failure in this node's communication with other nodes as default value is loopback address `localhost` hence node will not be able to communicate with other nodes running on different machines.

Default value: The default value is `localhost`.

`seed_provider`: The seed node helps Cassandra nodes to learn about other nodes in the cluster and ring topology using `Gossip` protocol. We'll learn more about Gossip protocol in later chapters. It has two suboptions, one is `class_name` and the other is number of seeds. The default seeding class takes a comma-delimited list of node addresses. In a multinode cluster, the seed list should have at least one node. This list should be common for all nodes.

Default value: The default value is `-class_name:org.apache.cassandra.locator.SimpleSeedProvider-seeds: "127.0.0.1"`.

The seed list should have more than one node for fault tolerance of the bootstrapping process.

In a multi-data center cluster, at least one node from each data center should participate as a seed node.

A node cannot be a seed node if it is a bootstrapping node. So, during the bootstrapping process, the node shouldn't be in the seeds list.

• Data partitioning

`num_tokens`: This configuration defines the number of random tokens this node will hold, hence defining the partitioning ranges that this node can hold. This is a relative configuration. For example, if a node has `num_tokens` as `128` while another node has `256`, then it means that the second node is handling twice the data partition ranges than the first node is handling.

Default value: The default value is `256`.

All nodes with the same hardware capability should have the same number of tokens configured.

`partitioner`: This defines the data partition algorithm used in the Cassandra cluster. The current default algorithm — Murmur3 — is very fast and is considered as a good data partition algorithm as compared to its predecessors. So, while forming a new cluster, you should go with the default value, which is `org.apache.cassandra.dht.Murmur3Partitioner`.

 This setting shouldn't be changed once the data is loaded, as changing this will wipe all data directories, hence deleting data.

- Storage configurations

  `data_file_directories`: Using this configuration option, we can set the data storage location.

    Default value: The default value is `$CASSANDRA_HOME/data/data/ var/lib/cassandra/data` in older versions.

  `commitlog_directory`: This is the location in HDD where Cassandra will store `commitlog`.

    Default value: The default value is `$CASSANDRA_HOME/data/ commitlog /var/lib/cassandra/commitlog` in older versions.

 If using non-SSDs, you should have a separate disk for storing `commitlog`. Commit logs are append-only logs, however data files are random seeks in nature; so, using the same disk will affect the write performance of commit logs. Also, commit logs disks can be smaller in size. As the `commitlog` space is reusable once flushed to Disk from Memtable.

  `saved_caches_directory`: This is the location where cached rows, partition keys, or counters will be saved to disk after a certain duration of time.

    Default value: The default value is $CASSANDRA_HOME/data/ saved_caches/var/lib/cassandra/saved_caches

 Row caching is disabled by default in `cassandra.yaml` due to its limited use.

- Client configurations

  `rpc_address`: This is the thrift RPC service bind interface. You should set it appropriately; using the default won't allow connections from outside the node.

    Default value: The default value is `localhost`.

`rpc_port`: This acts as a thrift service port.

Default value: The default value is `9160`

`native_transport_port`: This is the port on which the CQL native transport will listen for clients; for example, `cqlsh` or Java Driver. This will use `rpc_address` as the connection interface.

Default Value: The default value is `9042`.

- Security configurations

`authenticator`: This configuration is used to specify whether you want to use a password-based authentication or none. For password-based authentication, `authenticator` should be set to `PasswordAuthenticator`. If `PasswordAuthenticator` is used, a username and hashed password are saved in the `system_auth.credentials` table.

Default value: The default value is `AllowAllAuthenticator`, which means no authentication.

`authorizer`: This configuration is used if you want to limit permissions to Cassandra objects, for example, tables. To enable authorization, set its value to `CassandraAuthorizer`. If enabled, it stores authorization information in the `system_auth.pemissions` table.

Default value: The default value is `AllowAllAuthorizer`, which means authorization disabled.

 If enabling authentication or authorization, increase `system_auth` keyspace's replication factor.

- `cassandra-env.sh`

  This file can be used to fine-tune Cassandra. Here, you can set/tune a Java environement variable such as `MAX_HEAP_SIZE`, `HEAP_NEWSIZE`, and `JAVA_OPTS`.

- `cassandra-in.sh`

  Here, you can alter the default values for environment variables such as `JAVA_HOME`, `CASSANDRA_HOME` and `CLASSPATH`. Its location is in `$CASSANDRA_HOME/bin/` in binary tarball installations. Package-based installations put this file inside the `/user/share/cassandra` directory.

- `cassandra-rackdc.properties`

  The rack and data center configurations for a node are defined here. The default datacenter is `DC1` and the default rack is `RAC1`.

- `cassandra-topology.properties`

  This file contains mapping of Cassandra node IPs to data center and racks.

- `logback.xml`

  This file lets you configure the logging properties of Cassandra's `system.log`. It is not available in older versions of Cassandra.

Running a Cassandra server

Now that we know the prerequisites, let's quickly check the language dependencies:

We can check the Java version using the following code:

```
$ java -version
java version "1.7.0_45"
```

The Python version can be checked using this command:

```
$ python -version
Python 2.6.6
```

Running a Cassandra node

Since we're running only single node, we can skip configurations and directly start our node. Run the Cassandra node using the command for tarball installation:

```
$ bin/Cassandra
```

We can stop the server by using the following command:

```
$ pgrep -u `whoami` -f cassandra | xargs kill -9
```

Sometimes, we might want to run a Cassandra node in the foreground for debugging purposes, then we'll run it with `-f flag`:

```
$ bin/cassandra -f
```

To stop, press *Ctrl + C*.

For package-based installations, use the following commands to start and stop, respectively:

```
$ sudo service Cassandra start
$ sudo service Cassandra stop
```

Wohooo!! Our node is running, let's check our Cassandra server version:

```
$nodetool version
ReleaseVersion: 2.1.2
```

 Since we used the default Cassandra configuration, our node is running on the local interface and we'll not be able to connect to it from outside this machine using clients, for example, Java driver or other CQL clients.

Setting up the cluster

Let's set up a three-node cluster with the IPs 127.0.0.1, 127.0.0.2 and 127.0.0.3. So, our Cassandra.yaml for each node will look like this:

```
####### Cassandra Node 1 #######
cluster_name: 'Apache Cassandra Essentials'
num_tokens: 256
seed_provider:
    - class_name: org.apache.cassandra.locator.SimpleSeedProvider
      parameters:
            - seeds: "127.0.0.2"
listen_address: localhost
storage_port: 7000
####### Cassandra Node 2 #######
cluster_name: 'Apache Cassandra Essentials'
num_tokens: 256
seed_provider:
    - class_name: org.apache.cassandra.locator.SimpleSeedProvider
      parameters:
            - seeds: "127.0.0.2"
listen_address: 127.0.0.2
storage_port: 7000
####### Cassandra Node 3 #######
cluster_name: 'Apache Cassandra Essentials'
num_tokens: 256
seed_provider:
    - class_name: org.apache.cassandra.locator.SimpleSeedProvider
      parameters:
            - seeds: "127.0.0.2"
listen_address: 127.0.0.3
storage_port: 7000
```

Since all our nodes are the same from a hardware configuration perspective, we used `num_tokens: 256` for all of them. The second node with an IP address of `127.0.0.2` acts as a seed node.

Additionally, we can set `rpc_address` and `native_transport_ports` for each node so that our Java client can connect to our nodes.

Now, we'll run the Cassandra server on each node using as discussed in the previous section, and our cluster with three nodes is ready.

Viewing the cluster status

Now that our cluster is up and running, let's check its status. We can use the Cassandra tool called `nodetool` to check the status:

```
$ nodetool status
Datacenter: datacenter1

========================
Status=Up/Down
|/ State=Normal/Leaving/Joining/Moving
--  Address        Load        Tokens  Owns    Host ID
Rack
UN  127.0.0.1   171.88 MB      256      ?       940ba0cf-b75a-448c-a15e-
40e05efbeb34   rack1

UN  127.0.0.2   141.12 MB      256      ?       4b728c3c-c545-4e4d-b1aa-
2f66ef6bdce   rack1
UN  127.0.0.3   174.71 MB      256      ?       d63a18c4-0d2c-4574-8f66-
c4eb1e5ca5a8   rack1
Note: Non-system keyspaces don't have the same replication settings,
effective ownership information is meaningless
```

The first character in the status, which is U in our example, denotes the node's status whether it is Up (U) or Down (D). The second character tells us about the state of the joining cluster; it can be Normal (N), Leaving (L), Joining (J), or Moving (M). In our example, every node in the cluster is Up (U) and in the Normal (N) state. So, the first column is UN for each node. It also tells us about the data center in which our node lies. In our example, all the nodes lie in 'DataCenter 1' and rack 'rack1'.

Now, let's use the `nodetool info` command to check the individual node statistics such as its uptime, caching details, load details, and so on. We'll discuss Cassandra caching in detail in *Chapter 4, Read and Write – Behind the Scenes*:

```
$ nodetool info
ID              : 2f9bb0a9-db48-4146-83c6-4ce06bd22259
Gossip active   : true
```

```
Thrift active      : true
Native Transport active: true
Load               : 179.4 MB
Generation No      : 1422937400
Uptime (seconds)   : 593431
Heap Memory (MB)   : 474.63 / 920.00
Data Center        : datacenter1
Rack               : rack1
Exceptions         : 0
Key Cache          : entries 226, size 23.07 KB, capacity 45 MB, 4714 hits,
5006 requests, 0.942 recent hit rate, 14400 save period in seconds
Row Cache          : entries 0, size 0 bytes, capacity 600 MB, 0 hits, 0
requests, NaN recent hit rate, 3000 save period in seconds
Counter Cache      : entries 0, size 0 bytes, capacity 22 MB, 0 hits, 0
requests, NaN recent hit rate, 7200 save period in seconds
Token              : (invoke with -T/--tokens to see all 256 tokens)
```

Summary

Cassandra can be installed via various methods. We can install it on different platforms based on our requirements. However, platforms based on *NIX are very popular for production deployments. While deploying, we should consider various configuration options based on our deployment type. There are the configuration options that are used for performance tuning; we'll uncover more options later. The Cassandra nodetool is very handy to monitor and debug clusters and column families. We discussed some of them in this chapter.

In the next chapter, we'll see more of the nodetool options in more detail.

2

An Architectural Overview

Now we know how to set up and run a Cassandra cluster, so let's take another step and discuss the architecture of Cassandra. Cassandra is a highly available, distributed NoSQL database. Cassandra clusters can be linearly scalable depending on our load requirements. Cassandra has no single point of failure, as it allows us to control the trade-off between consistency and latency based on our requirements. In a Cassandra cluster, there is no master or slave — node all nodes are equal. This way enables Cassandra to read from any node and write to any node unlike some traditional relational databases. Cassandra partitions data among all nodes in its cluster; this partitioned data can be looked up using a key called a **partition key**. Cassandra replicates data among its cluster nodes to become highly available. We can configure data replication based on our specific requirements. In this chapter, we'll discuss more about these features of Cassandra.

Background

Cassandra's design was based on Google's **Bigtable** and Amazon's **DynamoDB**, and it was developed at Facebook. Later on, it was open sourced to Apache Foundation. It is a NoSQL nonrelational database. While working with Cassandra, we need not worry about normalization of our tables, as Cassandra promotes denormalization of your database tables. In Cassandra, the database schema is designed based on the data that you would be reading from or writing to Cassandra.

Cassandra focuses on availability and partition tolerance among consistency, availability, and partition tolerance of the CAP theorem by Brewer. The CAP theorem states that, among consistency, availability, and partition tolerance, you can pick only two at a time. Here, consistency means when you read from or write to any node of the cluster, you should get the same up-to-date data. Availability refers to the fact that we should be able to access the cluster even if some node in the cluster is down, and partition tolerance means our cluster should be functional even if communication between nodes of a cluster is broken.

Cassandra has the flexibility to allow us to choose either strong consistency or eventual consistency. Here, eventual consistency means that when a write operation is completed, data will be synced to all nodes of the cluster that are responsible to cater for this data, sooner or later. However, if we choose strong consistency, the latency increases.

Cassandra cluster overview

As mentioned earlier, Cassandra is a peer to peer cluster—no node is master or slave. Data is distributed among all nodes of the cluster using partitioners. This enables Cassandra to shard data transparently, and allows it to scale linearly. This means that Cassandra server performs the data sharding, and the application layer need not implement any additional logic for sharding. As the load grows, new nodes can be added to share the load as Cassandra will distribute the load among them automatically.

For example, let's imagine that we initially have three node cluster, which are capable of handling 3x transactions. Now, suppose that the load is increased to 4x, then we can add one additional node to the cluster without doing any change in our application layer. The following image shows the example where initially we have a three-node cluster with nodes A, B, and C capable of handling load 1x each; hence, the capacity of handling load of 1x + 1x + 1x = 3x. However, later on, we added one more node **D** of capacity 1x to our cluster. Now, our cluster can handle 3x + 1x = 4x load. Cassandra will automatically distribute data among the newly added fourth node as well, and this new node will start serving incoming requests of read and write:

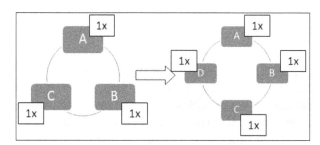

One of Cassandra's features is to replicate data for fault tolerance purposes. The number of replicas is configurable per keyspace level.

While working with a distributed, highly available database, one of the desirable features is data consistency. Here, consistency refers to the fact that if our data is replicated among various nodes, and we can read from and write to any node, then a read query sent to any of the node should always retrieve up-to-date data irrespective of which node received write query for latest data. In Cassandra, data becomes eventually consistent among all nodes, however, while reading or writing data we can configure consistency levels. Cassandra lets us control data consistency per-request basis to control trade-off between consistency and latency. This means we can decide whether we require strong consistency or relaxed consistency to achieve the required performance. For example, while adding items to a cart in a shopping cart scenario, we can use relaxed consistency, as here we prefer speed over strong consistency requirements for better user experience. For a financial transactions, we need a strong consistency; however, we might compromise on the latency here.

Cassandra stores data in the form of rows, which are accessed by a key called the partition key. A row is stored completely on a node. Cassandra allows us to read from or to write to any node. The node that is contacted for any read or write operation is called a **coordinator node**. Any node can act as a coordinator node.

The Gossip protocol

Cassandra nodes use the Gossip protocol to know about the location and state of other nodes in the cluster. Every node starts a gossipier task periodically, which is currently 1 second, to know the status of other nodes via gossip.

During a Gossip session. node selection is done as follows:

1. First, Gossip to some random live endpoint.
2. Then, Gossip to a random unreachable endpoint
3. If the node gossiped in step 1 is not a seed node, then gossip to a seed node.

A gossiping session constitutes three messages: DigestSyn, DigestAck, and DigestAck2. A typical gossip session stated by node **A** to some random node **B** is as shown in following figure. As we can see, node **A** first sends a DigestSyn message to node **B**. Upon receiving this message, node **B** replies with the DigestAck message, which contains a list of DigestMessage functions and a Map of EndpointState, which uses the node's IP address as a key. As we can see in the figure, node **A** finally completes the gossip session by sending the DigestAck2 message:

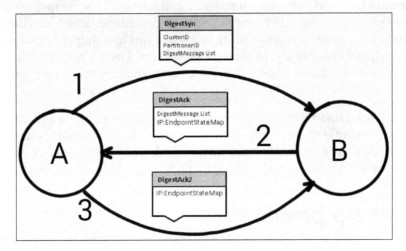

In the DisgestSyn message, a node sends three things to other node:

- Cluster id value which we've defined in its cassandra.yaml file
- The partitioner algorithm which is being used by the node and
- List of digest messages received from other nodes in previous Gossip session.

A DigestMessage is made up three entities, as shown in next figure:

- Endpoint IP address of the node to which this DigestMessage belongs
- Generation number which tells about node restart status; on node restarts generation number changes.
- Version number for digest message.

Let's have a look at the following screenshot:

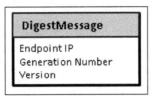

Every node maintains a list of structures called EndpointState, where it stores other nodes' heartbeat statuses. The heartbeat state is composed of the generation number and gossip message version number. The ApplicationState can be a node's status whether it's in normal state, bootstrapping, leaving cluster, or so on. The structure looks similar to following screenshot:

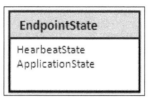

Let's assume that node **A** is gossiping to node **B** at any point of time. During that time, the local EndpointState map at node **A** might be as shown in the following figure:

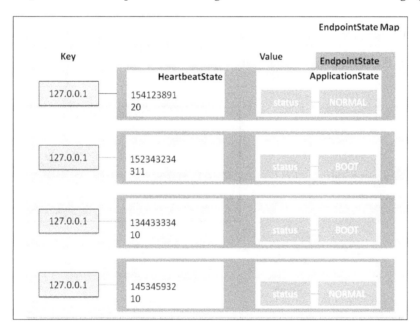

Now, node **A** starts the gossiping session by sending the `DigestSyn` message to node **B**, as shown in following figure:

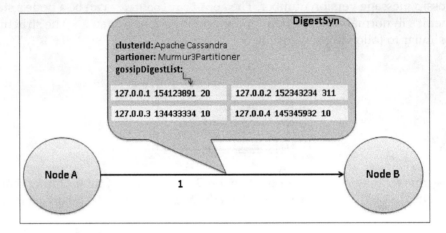

Node **B** receives `DigestSyn`. Let's assume that at that point of time, the local digest list at Node **B** is as shown in following figure:

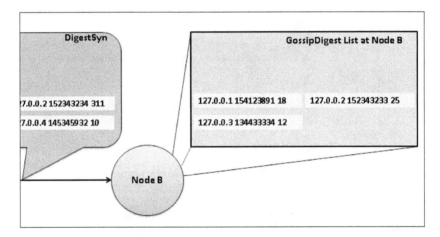

Node **B** sorts the list, and after calculating delta, it finds that for an endpoint with IP address `127.0.0.1`, the generation number is the same but the heartbeat version is older. So, it needs to ask node **A** to send all data above version 18 by appending the `DigestMessage 127.0.0.1:154123891:18` to list.

For the endpoint with IP address `127.0.0.2`, the generation number is changed. So, node **B** needs to ask node **A** to send all data above the generation number `152343234` whose version number is greater than 0 by adding the digest message `127.0.0.2:152343234:0`.

For an endpoint with IP address `127.0.0.3`, the generation numbers are the same, but node **B** has the latest version, so node **B** will have to send this data to node **A** by sending the `EndpoingState` message as `127.0.0.3:[134433334:12:['status':['Normal']]:['rack':[ 'rack1']]]`.

For a node with IP address `127.0.0.4`, node **B** doesn't have any data, so it needs to ask for all the data for this endpoint from node **A** by adding the digest message `127.0.0.4:145345932:0`.

The following image shows the final outgoing `DigestAck` message from node **B** toward node **A**:

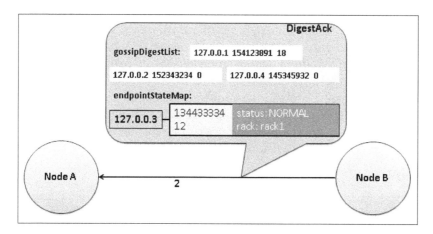

When node **A** receives `DigestAck`, it updates its record for `127.0.0.3` and sends all data for other nodes as requested by node **B** via `DigestAck2` message. This newly constructed `DigestAck2` message by node **A** to node **B** will look similar to the following image. This message will mark this Gossip session as complete:

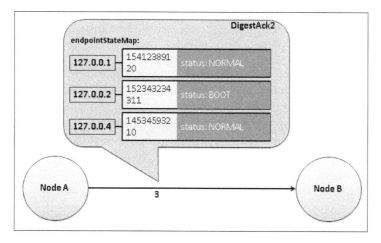

Failure detection

While gossiping with each other, Cassandra nodes track status of other nodes. Cassandra uses the phi accrual failure detector mechanism (which is elaborated at `http://www.jaist.ac.jp/~defago/files/pdf/IS_RR_2004_010.pdf`) to detect whether a node has failed. Unlike some methods of detecting node failure where a node is marked as dead if its heartbeats are missing for some hardcoded time, it marks a node as dead when it finds that the missed heartbeat values increase exponentially and reach a configured threshold. This means that if a node's heartbeat is missing during a gossip session, then it isn't marked as down immediately; instead, its phi value is incremented. This value keeps on increasing if subsequent heartbeats are missing, and the node will be marked down when a threshold is reached for the phi value. The `phi_convict_threshold` configuration option in `cassandra.yaml` serves as this threshold value. Detecting failures using this method helps Cassandra not to wrongly convict a node as dead if some heartbeats from the node are missed, in case the node is temporarily loaded for some time or some temporary network failures. The `phi_convict_threshold` allows us to tune the failure detector based on our environment; lower values will make a node's failure detection relatively aggressive than higher values. Higher values can be chosen in less reliable network environments or machines with resource contentions for a short duration of time.

The calculation of phi is done as follows:

$$\text{Phi Value} = \frac{T \text{ (Current Time)} - t_0 \text{ (Last Recorded Time when a HeartBeat was received)}}{M \text{ (Mean Heartbeat Inter Arrival Time from previously recorded samples)}}$$

Phi value is then multiplied by a magic number called `PHI_FACTOR` whose value is `~0.438`. If the multiplication product of the phi value with `PHI_FACTOR` becomes greater than the configured value of `phi_convict_threshold`, then the node is marked as dead.

Let's take an example of two nodes: node **A** and node **B**. Suppose node **B** is sending heartbeats to node **A** at regular intervals. Upon completing a Gossip session, node **A** is regularly counting phi value for node **B** heartbeats and checking whether it's less than the configured threshold or not. After some time, t_0, node **B** goes down, hence node **A** doesn't get any heartbeat afterwards. From this point onward, the phi value will start increasing. If node **B** doesn't comes back till the phi value crosses the configured threshold, then node **B** is marked dead by node **A**. This situation is shown in the following figure:

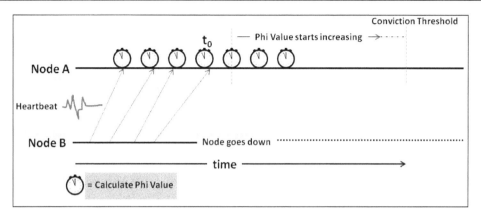

Data distribution

One of the key features of Cassandra is auto-sharding. Data is distributed among nodes in a cluster based on partition keys automatically. A partition key is a column or multiple columns, which are part of a primary key of a column family. Data is distributed based on the tokenized value calculated over the partition key. A partitioner determines how distribution tokens are calculated. Each node of Cassandra cluster its owns a range of tokens. A row is stored on the node that owns the respective token of the row's partition key.

A partitioner can be set using the configuration option partitioner in cassandra.yaml. The new cluster should go with Murmur3Partitioner, as it is a faster partitioner than older ones and also distributes data more efficiently. Other partitioners for backward compatibility are RandomPartitioner, ByteOrderedPartitioner, and OrderPreservingPartitioner.

Here is a brief description of all the listed partitioners:

- Murmur3Partitioner: This is the default partitioner. It calculates tokens based on the MurmurHash hash. The token value range from -2^{64} to $2^{64}-1$.

- RandomPartitioner: This is the previous default partitioner. Tokens are calculated based on the MD5 hash. The token value ranges from 0 to 2^{127}.

- ByteOrderedPartitioner: This is based on storing data in lexicographical order of partition key bytes. It is generally not recommended, as some partitions here are more active and can create hotspots. These hotspots will change as per workloads so managing them can be challenging.

- OrderPreservingPartitioner: It is similar to ByteOrderedPartitioner with the same challenges along with an additional limitation that it assumes that keys are UTF8 strings.

Let's discuss an example to understand data distribution using hash-based token generation, for example, `Murmur3Partitioner`. Suppose we have a column family named users with the username as partition key and a cluster of four nodes:

Username [Partition Key]	e-mail	Address
Jasper	`rnare.tortor@` `usissetqueneque.org`	309-8480 Sed Street
Nolan	`vestibulum.massa@` `morbi.ca`	P.O. Box 630, 9865 Ac, Street
Elton	`auctor.velit.Aliquam@` `vel.com`	409-4806 Ridiculus Rd.
Beau	`erat.neque.non@` `rtrumagna.net`	P.O. Box 656, 44 Libero. Av.

 Here, to avoid complexity while going through the example, we are not using the actual hash values for partition keys. Also, we are taking a very small token range, that is, -2³ to 2³-1, instead of -2⁶⁴ to 2⁶⁴-1, which is the actual token range.

The following table shows actual hash values and the imaginary hash values as an example:

Username [Partition Key]	Imaginary Hash Token	Actual Murmur3Hash token
Jasper	`1`	`1715133524295962640`
Nolan	`3`	`3030570987123988440`
Elton	`-8`	`-8167458529902320775`
Beau	`4`	`4065203685005646031`

The token range from `-8` to `7` is distributed among four nodes as shown in the following figure. Here, node **A** has tokens with values greater than or equal to `-8` and less than `-4`, node **B** has tokens for a range greater than or equal to `-4` and less than `0`, node **C** has tokens with value greater than or equal to `0` and less than `4`, and node **D** has a range greater than equal to `4` and less than `8`:

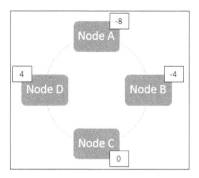

So, our first row whose partition key is Jasper with token value 1 will go to node **C** as node **C** owns that token range. Similarly, Nolan, Elton, and Beau will go to node **C**, node **A**, and node **D**, respectively.

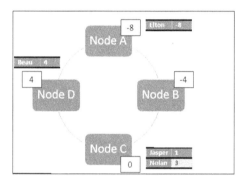

Replication

Cassandra is able to automatically keep multiple copies of data on multiple nodes, hence providing no single point of failure. The number of copies it will create is configurable and determined by a configuration option called a `replication_factor`. While defining a keyspace, we mention its `replication_factor` function. This configuration option is applied to all column families of that keyspace. Let's suppose that column family users, which we discussed in the section *Data distribution*, are part of the keyspace called `cassandrademodb`; and `replication_factor` of the keyspace is 3, then every row of the column family users will have three replicas copied to three different nodes. All replicas are the same and there is no primary or secondary replica. First, replica placement is decided by the partitioner and subsequent replicas are placed on consecutives nodes in clockwise order. Cassandra tries not to have two replicas on the same rack while doing so for rack-aware strategies, using snitch. Snitch is discussed in detail in the next section.

The value of `replication_factor` should not exceed the number of nodes in the cluster; otherwise, the write operations will start failing.

Cassandra has two replication strategy options; these strategies are applied and configured at keyspace level. So we mention them while creating a keyspace.

SimpleStrategy

The `SimpleStrategy` is a basic replication strategy. It's used when using a single datacenter. This method is rack unaware. It places replicas on subsequent nodes in a clockwise order.

Here is a sample CQL command to create a keyspace with `SimpleStrategy` and a replication factor of 3, which can be fired from the `cqlsh` prompt:

```
cqlsh>  CREATE KEYSPACE cassandrademodb WITH REPLICATION = { 'class' :
'SimpleStrategy', 'replication_factor' : 3 };
```

NetworkTopologyStrategy

The `NetworkTopologyStrategy` lets you define how many replicas would be placed in different datacenters, hence making it suitable for multidata center deployments. It's a rack-aware replication strategy, so it tries to avoid two replicas to be placed on the same rack. So, if one rack fails, another replica is available on a different rack in the datacenter and we need not to go to different datacenter for the replica. In this strategy, the sum of the datacenter replication factor is the effective replication factor for the keyspace. For example, if we have two datacenters, `dc1` and `dc2`, with replication factor 3 and 2, respectively, then the replication factor of the keyspace will be 5.

We can create a keyspace with `NetworTopologyStrategy` and a replication factor of 5 with two datacenters `dc1` and `dc2`, as follows:

```
cqlsh> CREATE KEYSPACE cassandrademodb WITH REPLICATION = {'class' :
'NetworkTopologyStrategy', 'dc1' : 3, 'dc2' : 2};
```

 Here, `dc1` should have total number of nodes more than three and `dc2` more than two; otherwise, the write request will fail.

 While using `NetworkTopologyStrategy`, we should change the snitch from `SimpleSnitch` to `GossipPropertyFileSnitch` or to another rack-aware snitch.

Snitches

Snitch is a mechanism that Cassandra nodes employ to know the relative proximity of other nodes for effective routing of requests. For example, it can help to know where to put replicas of a row and to avoid putting them on the same rack, if possible. The following are some snitch mechanisms that can be configured in the `cassandra.yaml` file under the configuration option `endpoint_snitch`.

- `SimpleSnitch`: This is suitable for single datacenter deployment. It doesn't know anything about the datacenter or rack. The order in keyspace replication strategy will be used for proximity consideration.

- `GossipingPropertyFileSnitch`: This is advisable to use for production purposes. It uses the configuration file `cassandra-rackdc.properties` for reading rack and datacenter information. It also uses the `cassandra-topology.properties` file for compatibility with `PropertyFileSnitch` in case of migrations.

Let's take an example of a Cassandra cluster with total nine nodes in two data centers. Assume the first data center has five nodes and second has four nodes. Let's name our datacenters with names DC1 and DC2 for datacenter 1 and datacenter 2 respectively. Now suppose for the first datacenter DC1 we are placing node 1, node 5 and node 4 in one rack and node 2 and node 3 in a second rack, suppose we're denoting our racks with names RACK1 and RACK2 for the first and second rack respectively then `cassandra-rackdc.properties` file for node 1, node 5 and node 4 will have entries like follows:

```
dc=DC1
rack=RACK1
```

And for node 2 and node 3 these entries will look like:

```
dc=DC1
rack=RACK2
```

Similarly for second datacenter DC2 if we're placing nodes node one and node four in RACK1 and node two and node three in second rack RACK2 then configuration for node one and node four will be like:

```
dc=DC2
rack=RACK1
```

And for node two and node three it'll be:

```
dc=DC2
rack=RACK2
```

Let's take a look at the graphical representation of the preceding example Cassandra cluster:

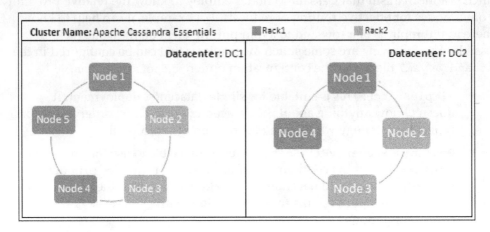

Here is a brief description of the entire listed Snitch:

- `PropertyFileSnitch`: This uses `cassandra-topology.properties` for rack and datacenter information.

- `Ec2Snitch`: This is appropriate if the Cassandra cluster is in the Amazon EC2 cloud in a single region. A region is treated as a datacenter. It uses private IPs of the cloud machines.

- `Ec2MultiRegionSnitch`: This is the same as the preceding Snitch, but this is appropriate if the cluster is in different Amazon EC2 regions. It uses public IPs for crossregion talks.

- `RackInferringSnitch`: This uses IP address octets of each node for considering them on different racks and datacenters. The second octet is used to determine the datacenter and the third octet is used to determine the rack.

Let's take a look at the following figure:

	Datacenter	Rack	
172	16	128	15

Virtual nodes

In earlier versions of Cassandra, prior to version 1.2, each node used to own only one token, and hence it was responsible for handling only one contiguous token range in the cluster ring. This mechanism was good but was slower and relatively harder to configure in following scenarios:

- Configuring a cluster.

   While configuring a cluster, we need to calculate and assign tokens to each node manually.

- Adding or removing a node

   When a node is added or removed, we need to do a token calculation again to rebalance the cluster. If a node is added, we need to assign a new token range to this node and reduce the token range of the rest of the nodes. Similarly, if a node is removed, we need to calculate the token range again so that a larger token range is handled by each node.

- Replacing a dead node.

   Prior to virtual nodes each node was responsible for handling a big contiguous token range. When such a node is dead and replaced by a new node, other node/s responsible for same token range will start pumping the data to this new replacement node. Since token range is big and lesser number of nodes used to participate in this process so this process used to take longer and used to put more pressure on those nodes.

Newer Cassandra release, release 1.2 and later, introduced a new mechanism called virtual nodes. In this mechanism, unlike the previous mechanism, every Cassandra cluster node can own multiple tokens instead of only one token. Hence, each node owns smaller noncontiguous token ranges. In a way, a single Cassandra node is acting like multiple virtual nodes of previous versions.

While using virtual nodes, the replica of a partition is copied to the next virtual node, which might not be on the same physical machine. This is somewhat similar to NetworkTopologyStrategy, where Cassandra tries not to place a replica on the same rack.

Now, during configuration of new cluster, we no longer calculate token ranges and assign them to nodes; instead, we just specify how many random token ranges it'll own. Hence, rebalancing of nodes is not required when adding or removing a node.

If we want some node to handle more load as it has more powerful hardware than other nodes, then we can assign that node more `num_tokens`. So, that node will have a larger token range than other nodes.

While replacing a dead node, the bootstrap time is reduced as more number of nodes are now participating while pumping data to the replacement node. Also, the amount of data that is being pumped by each node is lesser due to smaller token ranges, hence making this process faster.

To configure virtual nodes, Cassandra introduces a configuration option called `num_tokens` in `cassandra.yaml`. Its default value is `256`, so with this value, a node is handling 256 small randomly assigned token ranges. To use the older functionality, we can use the `initial_token` configuration option in `cassandra.yaml`, which will override this option.

Adding nodes to our cluster

Now, let's extend our node to a five-node cluster from a three-node cluster. Let's take two new loopback IPs as `127.0.0.4` and `127.0.0.5`.

 Here, we're using loopback IPs for the simplicity of our example; if you're running using the same on a single machine, ensure that it has enough RAM and CPU on the host machine.

The `cassandra.yaml` file with key configuration options for these two new nodes will look as follows:

```
####### Cluster Node 4 #######
cluster_name: 'Apache Cassandra Essentials'
auto_bootstrap: true
num_tokens: 256
seed_provider:
    - class_name: org.apache.cassandra.locator.SimpleSeedProvider
      parameters:
          - seeds: "127.0.0.2"
listen_address: 127.0.0.4
storage_port: 7000
endpoint_snitch: GossipingPropertyFileSnitch
```

A sample `cassandra.yaml` file for node 5 with some key configuration parameters is shown in the following image. Here, both the nodes are using node 2 with the IP address `127.0.0.2` as the seed node:

```
####### Cluster Node 5 #######
cluster_name: 'Apache Cassandra Essentials'
auto_bootstrap: true
num_tokens: 256
seed_provider:
    - class_name: org.apache.cassandra.locator.SimpleSeedProvider
      parameters:
          - seeds: "127.0.0.2"
listen_address: 127.0.0.5
storage_port: 7000
endpoint_snitch: GossipingPropertyFileSnitch
```

In the preceding figure, we've enabled `auto_bootstrap` for both the nodes so that data will be automatically migrated to these nodes for the token range they'll own. Also, as we can see that we're using the snitch type `GossipingPropertyFileSnitch` in the images, let's update the `cassandra-rackdc.properties` files for each node. Let's assume node 1, node 4, and node 5 are in RAC1, and node 2 and node 3 are in RAC2, and all are in the same datacenter DC1. The `cassandra-rackdc.properties` for node 1 will look like as follows:

```
##### casandra-rackdc.properties Node 1 ######
dc=DC1
rack=RAC1
```

Node 2 is in the same datacentre but in a different rack, so its property file will look as shown in following image:

```
##### casandra-rackdc.properties Node 2 ######
dc=DC1
rack=RAC2
```

Node 3 will have the same settings that were done for node 2. The following image snapshot lists configuration for node 3:

```
##### casandra-rackdc.properties Node 3 ######
dc=DC1
rack=RAC2
```

Here is the configuration for node 4; the settings are the same as we did for node 1:

```
##### casandra-rackdc.properties Node 4 ######
dc=DC1
rack=RAC1
```

The following image lists the configurations that are needed to be done in the
`cassandra-rackdc.properties` file for node 5:

```
##### casandra-rackdc.properties Node 5 ######
dc=DC1
rack=RAC1
```

Now, start Cassandra for each node. After all the nodes are running, execute the
nodetool cleanup on node 1, node 2, and node 3 to remove the partitions that are
no longer owned by them. These partitions are now distributed to node 4 and node
5 during the bootstrap process. While we're running the cleanup on one node, we
should wait for its completion and then run the command on the next node.

Create keyspace and column family

Now, let's create our keyspace and a column family using the `cqlsh` client. Run the
command `cqlsh`, then you should be on the `cqlsh` prompt. On the `cqlsh` prompt,
run the keyspace creation command as follows:

```
cqlsh> CREATE KEYSPACE cassandrademodb WITH REPLICATION = { 'class' :
'SimpleStrategy', 'replication_factor' : 3 };
```

Here, we created a keyspace named `cassandrademodb`. We chose the replication
factor as 3, so each data row we'll be creating will be stored on three nodes. Since, for
now we're running our cluster on only one cluster, we chose the replication strategy
as `SimpleStrategy`.

Now, create one column family called `users` in this keyspace. Here, we'll use
username column as the partition key. Using the `cqlsh` prompt we can create
it as follows:

```
cqlsh> use cassandrademodb;
cqlsh:cassandrademodb> CREATE TABLE songs ( username text PRIMARY KEY,
email text, address text );
```

Here, we defined the username as a partition key as well as a primary key. However,
it's not necessary that a partition key must be a primary key. We'll see this in detail in
the next chapters.

Summary

In this chapter, we discovered various features of Cassandra that make it an ultrafast, highly available, distributed database with no single point of failure. We discussed how these features are achieved by Cassandra internally, for example, we discussed how data is distributed and then replicated among nodes of a Cassandra cluster. We discussed various replication strategies that are available with Cassandra and the criteria to choose one. We also discussed various data distribution algorithms available with Cassandra. We saw how the vnodes feature in Cassandra enables more efficient data distribution and load sharing among nodes. In the next chapters, we'll discuss in detail how Cassandra does a read/write operation internally and the data structures it has to server a read/write request. We'll also discuss the various techniques it uses to persist data and the uses of various techniques such as caching or compaction to make our queries faster.

3

Creating Database
and Schema

In the previous chapter, we learned about creating a keyspace and defining its replication strategy. In this chapter, we'll discuss how we can create tables in our keyspace. We'll see what different table options could be used while creating a table. We'll discuss various features provided by Cassandra, such as lightweight transactions and batch statements, and their trade-offs. Terms such as memtable, bloomfilter, index interval, and so on that we come across in this chapter will be discussed in detail in the next chapter.

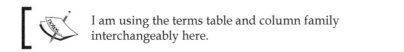

[I am using the terms table and column family interchangeably here.]

A database and schema

A Cassandra database schema has two major building blocks: Keyspace, Column Family and Primary Key for Column Family. Let's discuss them in some detail.

Keyspace

In previous chapters we learned that similar to RDBMS database Cassandra Keyspace is a namespace that logically contains a set of tables. A keyspace has there configuration options;

- Replication Strategy
- Replication Factor
- The `durable_writes`

Former two options we already discussed in previous chapter. The durable_writes option lets you to enable or disable the option of using commit log for updates. By default `durable_writes` is enabled and its suggested to keep this enabled.

We know how to create a keyspace but what if the keyspace already exists. in such case Cassandra will return error. However we can use `IF NOT EXISTS` option to disable error; using `IF NOT EXISTS` option Cassandra will do nothing if keyspace exists otherwise it'll create it:

```
CREATE KEYSPACE IF NOT EXISTS cassandrademodb WITH replication =
{'class': 'SimpleStrategy', 'replication_factor': '3'}  AND durable_
writes = true
```

Using the `USE <keyspace>` syntax for a keyspace lets us perform operations on that keyspace without explicitly mentioning it, for example:

```
USE cassandrademodb
```

Now, until we explicitly mention the target keyspace, every operation will be performed on the `cassandrademodb` keyspace.

The `ALTER` statement could be used to modify keyspace options such as replication strategy or replication factor, as shown in the following code:

```
ALTER KEYSPACE cassandrademodb WITH replication = {'class':
'SimpleStrategy', 'replication_factor': '4'}
```

> Altering the replication strategy or replication factor of a keyspace should be done with care as it might cause data inconsistencies in the cluster.
>
> **nodetool repair** should be run on each node in the cluster after altering replication. Also, we should wait until one node has been repaired and only then move to the next node in the cluster to run a `repair` command.

The `DROP` statement on a keyspace will delete a keyspace and all the column families it contains:

```
DROP KEYSPACE cassandrademodb
```

Column families

A column family stores the data in the form of rows and columns. A Cassandra row is identified by a row key, also called a **partition key**. Cassandra row could have one or more logical rows. These logical rows are identified by column family's primary key. The primary key of a column family must be unique. In next section of chapter we'll see that a primary key is composed of partition key and zero or more clustering columns. Cassandra row which can have only one logical row is called a static row and if Cassandra row can have one or more logical rows then it is called a wide row. The Static rows and wide rows are discussed in more detail in next section. partition key decides on which node all logical rows for that partition key will reside. This implies that a Cassandra row of a given partition key value always resides completely on a Cassandra node with all of its logical rows on the same node however Cassandra rows with different partition key values might or might not reside on same Cassandra node.

A row is comprised of columns, and a column has two parts: column name and column value. In a row, columns are sorted by column names, as shown in the following figure:

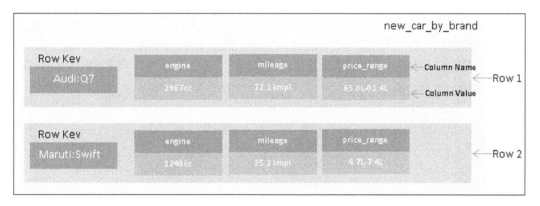

For example, in the preceding figure, we have a column family named `new_car_by_brand`. It has two rows. Each row has a row key defined by the column's brand and model, for example, Audi:Q7 and Maruti:Swift. Each row has three columns with the names engine, mileage, and price_range. Also we could see that column values are stored sorted based on column names.

The CREATE TABLE statement is used to create a table. In addition to column, column types, and primary key definition, a table has the options shown in the following table. If we don't specify these options during table creation, the respective default values are used.

Option	Description
bloom_filter_ fp_chance	This describes the probability of SSTable bloom filters giving false positives. The default value is 0.01. The smaller it is, the smaller the chances of giving false positives. For example, 0.01 means there is a 1 percent chance that the bloom filter might give a false positive for a partition key.
Caching	This option defines which caching options are enabled for the column family. It also defines how many rows to cache per partition key for each row cache. It can have the following values: • ALL: Both key cache and row cache are enabled. • KEYS_ONLY: Only key cache is enabled. • ROWS_ONLY: Only row cache is enabled. • None: Caching is disabled.
Comment	Any comment describing the table or other related information.
Compaction	This defines the compaction strategy and its options.
Compression	This defines the table compression properties such as the compression algorithm to use.
dclocal_read_ repair_chance	This describes the probability of querying extra nodes for read repair purposes in a datacenter.
default_time_ to_live	This describes the default expiration time for rows in a table. The default value is 0, which means never.
gc_grace_ seconds	This describes the wait time before the garbage collection process will clean tombstones.
min_index_ interval max_index_ interval	This configuration defines the sampling of keys from an on-disk primary index to in-memory IndexSummary. Unlike older versions, versions of Cassandra from 2.1 onwards don't fix the sampling interval to a value. Instead, this value can vary based on table usage between a range defined by min_index_ interval and max_index_interval. For a frequently used table, IndexSummary will be upsampled to the value of min_index_ interval, and for lesser used tables it'll be down sampled to the value of max_index_interval. The default value of min_index_ interval is 128 and that of max_index_interval is 2048.
memtable_flush_ period_in_ms	This option allows you to specify after an interval of how many milliseconds memTable will be flushed to disk.

Option	Description
read_repair_ chance	This describes the probability of querying extra nodes for read repair purposes. For example, a value of 0.01 means 1 percent requests will invoke background read repair. The default is 0.0.
speculative_ retry	This configuration option tells Cassandra when to send a retry request to another node if the node currently being used is down or slow.
	For example, if it is set to 10 ms and the response of a read request isn't received within 10 milliseconds, the coordinator node will send an additional request to another node. If that node had responded, the read timeout could have been avoided.
	It can have the following values:
	• ALWAYS: Always send additional retry requests.
	• Nms: A retry will be attempted if the contacted node doesn't respond within N milliseconds.
	• XPercentile: A retry will be attempted if the contacted node doesn't respond within the time recorded for X percent of past requests.
	• None: No retry.

The following is an example of creating a table by switching the value of the gc_grace_seconds option to 864000 (10 days) from 8640000 (100 days):

```
CREATE TABLE status_updates_by_user( userid text, updated_on
timestamp, status text, PRIMARY KEY (userid, updated_on)) WITH gc_
grace_seconds = 864000
```

A column family in Cassandra can have two types of rows, skinny or static rows and wide rows. Let's discuss them in detail.

Static rows

A static row has a fixed number of columns. A column family with no clustering key will always have a fixed number of rows per partition key, hence this is called a skinny row table. Here is an example of a table with skinny rows:

```
CREATE TABLE schemabuilder.users (
userid text PRIMARY KEY,
address text,
alternate_phone text,
firstname text,
lastname text,
primary_phone text
)
```

```
INSERT INTO users (userid, address, firstname , lastname , primary_
phone ) VALUES ( 'gaurav', 'sec-9 delhi', 'gaurav', 'pandey',
'142233');
INSERT INTO users (userid, address, firstname ,lastname , primary_
phone, alternate_phone ) VALUES ( 'nitinp', 'sec-15', 'nitin',
'padalia', '112233', '554422');
SELECT * FROM users ;

userid | address      | alternate_phone | firstname | lastname |
primary_phone
--------+-------------+-----------------+----------+----------+-----
----------
gaurav | sec-9 delhi |            null |   gaurav |   pandey |
142233
nitinp |      sec-15 |          554422 |    nitin |  padalia |
112233
```

Here, each partition key (userid, in this case) can have only one row.

Wide rows

Wide rows can have a variable number of rows per partition key. A column family with clustering columns can have variable rows per partition key. For example, a column family of status updates from a user with userid as the row key and status_update_time as the clustering key can have multiple logical rows per Cassandra row key for a given partition key, as follows:

```
CREATE TABLE user_status_updates (
useridtext,
status_update_time timestamp,
status_msg text,
PRIMARY KEY (userid, status_update_time)
)
// Insert two row with same row key
INSERT INTO user_status_updates (userid, status_update_time ,status_
msg ) VALUES ( 'nitinp', '2015-03-02 10:00:02', 'hello world')
INSERT INTO user_status_updates (userid, status_update_time ,status_
msg ) VALUES ( 'nitinp', '2015-01-02 10:00:02', 'good morning all')
SELECT * FROM user_status_updates ;

userid | status_update_time       | status_msg
--------+--------------------------+------------------
nitinp | 2015-01-02 10:00:02+0530 | good morning all
nitinp | 2015-03-02 10:00:02+0530 |      hello world
```

Let's have a look at the following figure:

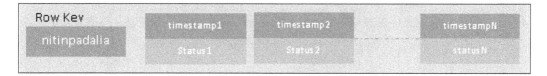

A primary key

In a column family, a row is uniquely identified by a primary key. It is mandatory for all column families to define a primary key. A primary key is comprised of partition keys and clustering columns. A single column primary key that only has a partition key is known as both primary key and partition key as well. All the rows of a partition key lie on a single node and are stored and sorted based on the clustering column.

Partition keys and clustering columns

The order of columns in a primary key identifies which columns act as partition keys and which as clustering columns. For example, in the following table, the very first column (`userid`) is the partition key and the second column (`status_update_time`) is a clustering column:

```
CREATE TABLE user_status_updates (
useridtext,
status_update_time timestamp,
status_msg text,
PRIMARY KEY (userid, status_update_time)
)
```

A composite partition key

It is possible to have more than one column as a partition key. In such cases, these columns are grouped inside parentheses to form a composite partition key, for example:

```
CREATETABLE cars(
brand text,
model text,
colors set<text>,
mileage decimal,
PRIMARY KEY((brand, model), variant)
)
```

Here, the brand and model columns form a composite partition key.

Multiple clustering columns

A table can have multiple clustering columns. These column values are sorted based on their ordering while defining the tale. Let's consider the following games tables:

```
CREATE TABLE games (
player text,
played_on timestamp,
overall_scoreint,
campaign text,
PRIMARY KEY (player,played_on, overall_score)
)
INSERT INTO games (player, played_on ,overall_score , campaign )
VALUES ( 'nitin' , '2013-10-12', 238 , 'Shotgun rain');
INSERT INTO games (player, played_on ,overall_score , campaign )
VALUES ( 'nitin' , '2013-10-12', 218 , 'Shotgun rain');
INSERT INTO games (player, played_on ,overall_score , campaign )
VALUES ( 'nitin' , '2013-10-12', 258 , 'Shotgun rain');
INSERT INTO games (player, played_on ,overall_score , campaign )
VALUES ( 'nitin' , '2013-10-11', 358 , 'Lets get it started');
INSERT INTO games (player, played_on ,overall_score , campaign )
VALUES ( 'nitin' , '2013-10-11', 328 , 'Lets get it started');
INSERT INTO games (player, played_on ,overall_score , campaign )
VALUES ( 'nitin' , '2013-10-11', 628 , 'Lets get it started');
```

In this example, the `player` column is a partition key and `played_on` and `overall_score` are clustering keys. Here, for a given player, data will be stored, sorted first by the date on which the game was played and then score-wise for a particular day. This can be seen in the following code:

```
SELECT * FROM games WHERE player = 'nitin';

player | played_on                 | overall_score | campaign
--------+---------------------------+---------------+-----------------
----
nitin | 2013-10-11 00:00:00+0530 |          328 | Lets get it started
nitin | 2013-10-11 00:00:00+0530 |          358 | Lets get it started
nitin | 2013-10-11 00:00:00+0530 |          628 | Lets get it started
nitin | 2013-10-12 00:00:00+0530 |          218 |         Shotgun rain
nitin | 2013-10-12 00:00:00+0530 |          238 |         Shotgun rain
nitin | 2013-10-12 00:00:00+0530 |          258 |         Shotgun rain
```

Static columns

Static columns are columns that are shared by all the rows of a partition key. We can declare some columns as static if they are expected to be the same for all clustered rows for the partition key. A column is declared as static by appending the keyword static after its type. For example, in a player profile by match type table, the team name of the player could be static as the team name doesn't change and will remain the same, as shown in the following example:

```
CREATE TABLE player_profile_by_matche_type (
player text,
match_type text,
match_playedint,
runsint,
highest_scoreint,
team text static,
PRIMARY KEY (player, match_type)
)
INSERT INTO player_profile_by_matche_type (player, match_type, match_
played, runs, highest_score, team) VALUES ('MS Dhoni', 'Tests', 90,
4876, 224, 'India')
// Since Team name is static so for second insert we don't mention it
explicitely
INSERT INTO player_profile_by_matche_type (player, match_type, match_
played, runs, highest_score) VALUES ('MS Dhoni', 'ODIs', 262, 8499,
183)
SELECT * FROM player_profile_by_matche_type WHERE player = 'MS Dhoni'
player   | match_type | team  | highest_score | match_played | runs
----------+------------+-------+---------------+--------------+------
MS Dhoni |       ODIs | India |           183 |          262 | 8499
MS Dhoni |      Tests | India |           224 |           90 | 4876
```

Note that, in preceding queries, even though we didn't mention, team in the second INSERT query, Cassandra shows the team as India for both rows. This is because the team column is a static column and bound to the row key player, which is MS Dhoni in this case.

Modifying a table

After creating a table, we can add or delete columns if required using the ALTER statement. ALTER also provides the option to change the type of a column. Table options can also be changed using ALTER as follows:

```
ALTER TABLE cars ADD newcol text
ALTER TABLE cars ALTER newcol TYPE varchar
ALTER TABLE cars DROP newcol
ALTER TABLE cars WITH gc_grace_seconds = '86400'
```

[We cannot change the type of clustering or secondary indexed columns.]

Table data can be dropped without deleting the table by using the TRUNCATE statement:

```
TRUNCATE cars
```

The table can be dropped by using the DROP statement:

```
DROP TABLE cars
```

Data types

Cassandra has five categories or data types:

1. **Native types**: These are built-in types in Cassandra. For each type there is a keyword to define.

2. **Collection types**: These types can store a group of native type elements. There are three categories — set, list, and map.

3. **Tuple types**: Tuple types can store a fixed length group of elements in a column similar to user-defined types, except that the tuple element field has no names. Hence, the ordering should be the same as during inserting a record in the order they are defined at table creation time. The following is an example of creating a column family with a tuple type:

```
CREATE TABLE user_reviews (
useriduuid PRIMARY KEY,
review frozen<tuple<text, text, decimal>>
)
INSERT INTO user_reviews (userid, review ) VALUES ( 9b02528d-75af-
41d9-866e-75d189f57118, ('awesome', 'This App is awesome', 4.8))
// Below will raise error due to wrong insertion order
INSERT INTO user_reviews (userid, review ) VALUES ( 9b02528d-75af-
41d9-866e-75d189f57118, (4.8, 'awesome', 'This App is awesome'))
```

4. **User Defined Types (UDT)**: In newer versions of Cassandra, we can define our custom types using other types. We'll discuss more about this later in the UDT section. UDT are supported in CQL specification version 3.2.0 and above.

5. **Custom types using a Java class**: We can also use a string as a type, which should resolve to a fully qualified Java class loadable by Cassandra. The Java class would extend `org.apache.cassandra.db.marshal.AbstractType`, for example, as in the following code:

```
CREATE TABLE my_custom_type (useriduuid, my_custom_type 'my.
example.cassandra.types.MyCustomType', PRIMARY KEY (userid))
```

Counters

The counter type is used to define counter columns. A counter column can either be incremented or decremented. Counter columns can be used to generate metrics information for some applications, for example, in a car search application; we might want to log how many users searched for a car model of a specific brand. In such a scenario, we could have a counter column family implemented in the following code:

```
CREATE TABLE car_search_counter (
brand text,
model text,
search_count counter,
    PRIMARY KEY ((brand, model))
)
```

Now whenever a user searches in the new_car_by_brand table, we should update the search_count field as well. For example, if a user searched for the Audi brand and model Q1, the following query could be run in addition to the search query:

```
UPDATE car_search_counter SET search_count = search_count + 1 WHERE
brand = 'Audi' and model = 'Q1'
```

Later on, we could get the metric about how many searches were done for Audi Q1 by using the following query:

```
SELECT search_count FROM car_search_counter WHERE brand = 'Audi' AND
model = 'Q1'
```

Counter columns have the following limitations:

- A primary key column cannot be defined as a counter type.
- A column family with a counter column can only have counter as a column type other than a primary key.
- We cannot perform the INSERT operation on a counter; fresh records are also inserted using UPDATE.
- Deletion of a counter row could result in undetermined behavior in certain scenarios. For resetting purposes, decrement the counter by its current value.
- Counter column removal is also not suggested.

Collections

Collections can be used to store multiple values in a cell. They should be used for relatively small amounts of data. If the number of elements in the column could grow unbounded, we should not use collections because collections are read at once and we cannot read more than the first 65535 elements from a collection column. Cassandra supports three collection types, which are outlined in the following subsections.

Sets

A set stores `uniqueelements` in sorted order; duplicate values are omitted. A table with a set can be created as follows:

```
CREATE TABLE cars(
brand text,
model text,
variant text,
colors set<text>,
mileage decimal,
PRIMARY KEY((brand, model), variant)
)
```

To `INSERT` values into a set, use comma separated values enclosed in curly brackets. An `INSERT` operation replaces the set:

```
INSERT INTO cars (brand, model, variant, colors, mileage) VALUES (
'ACME', 'S10 2.0WD MT', 'petrol', {'Golden Brown', 'Pearl White', 'Red
Pearl', 'Silver', 'Titanium'},
 13.8)
```

New elements can be added by using the `UPDATE` statement and + operator
as follows:

```
UPDATE cars SET colors = colors + {'Apple Green'}WHERE brand = 'ACME'
AND model = 'S10 2.0WD MT' AND variant = 'petrol'
```

The `UPDATE` statement with the – operator will remove elements from the set:

```
UPDATE cars SET colors = colors - {'Silver'}WHERE brand = 'ACME' AND
model = 'S10 2.0WD MT' AND variant = 'petrol'
```

All the elements of a set can be removed as follows:

```
UPDATE cars SET colors = { }WHERE brand = 'ACME' AND model = 'S10
2.0WD MT' AND variant = 'petrol'
Or
DELETE colors FROM cars WHERE brand = 'ACME' AND model = 'S10 2.0WD
MT' AND variant = 'petrol'
```

A set column with no elements will return `null`:

```
SELECT * FROM cars;

brand | model         | variant | colors | mileage
------+---------------+---------+--------+---------
  ACME | S10 2.0WD MT | petrol  |  null  |   13.8
```

Lists

Unlike sets, columns defined as lists can have non-unique values. Also, list elements are not sorted by value; instead, they are sorted by position. A list allows updating or removing an element by its position in the list. So, the list could be used in a situation where duplicate elements could exist and their insertion order is important. The following example will create a column family with `wickets_taken` as the list column:

```
CREATE TABLE bowler_performance_by_series (
bowler_id  uuid,
series text,
name text static,
team text static,
wickets_taken list<int>,
PRIMARY KEY (bowler_id, series)
)
```

The values in a `List` column can be set via putting elements in square brackets:

```
INSERT INTO bowler_performance_by_series (bowler_id, series ,wickets_
taken, name ) VALUES ( aa71ab3b-f9bb-4918-89f1-5c7579347773, 'India vs
Ireland', [1, 1, 2], 'Mohammed Shami')
```

A new element can be added either at the start or end of a list:

```
UPDATE bowler_performance_by_series SET wickets_taken = wickets_taken+
[0]WHEREbowler_id=  aa71ab3b-f9bb-4918-89f1-5c7579347773 AND series =
'India vs Ireland'
Or
UPDATE bowler_performance_by_series SET wickets_taken = [2] + wickets_
taken WHERE bowler_id = aa71ab3b-f9bb-4918-89f1-5c7579347773 and
series = 'India vs Ireland'
```

Individual elements in the list can be set as follows (this example will replace the very first element of the list with the value 3):

```
UPDATE bowler_performance_by_series SET wickets_taken[0] = 3 WHERE
bowler_id = aa71ab3b-f9bb-4918-89f1-5c7579347773 and series = 'India
vs Ireland';
```

We can use the – operator to remove all occurrences of a specific column value. The following example will remove all occurrences of 1 from the `wickets_taken` list for the player:

```
UPDATE bowler_performance_by_series SET wickets_taken= wickets_taken
- [1] WHERE bowler_id = aa71ab3b-f9bb-4918-89f1-5c7579347773 and
series = 'India vs Ireland'
```

> Setting or removing an element by its position and deleting all occurrences of the element's operations does a "read before write operation", so these operations are heavier performance wise.

> If there is no element duplication required and the insertion order of elements is not important, we should choose sets over lists as lists have performance implications for some operations.

Map

Using a map column, we can store elements in JSON-style key-value pairs. The sorting of elements is done based on keys:

```
CREATE TABLE player_batting_averages( player_iduuid, match_type text,
player_name text static, team text static, averages map<text, int>,
PRIMARY KEY (player_id, match_type)  )
```

Here, we can put in player averages for different match types as follows:

```
INSERT INTO player_batting_averages (player_id, match_type
,player_name , team , averages ) VALUES ( 9b02528d-75af-41d9-866e-
75d189f57118, 'Tests', 'AB de Villers', 'Sou
th Africa', { 'Matches': 98, 'Runs': 7606, 'Highest Score': 278})
INSERT INTO player_batting_averages (player_id, match_type
,player_name , team , averages ) VALUES ( 9b02528d-75af-41d9-866e-
75d189f57118, 'ODIs', 'AB de Villers', 'Sout
h Africa', { 'Matches': 187, 'Runs': 7941, 'Highest Score': 162})
```

We can update new statistics for **one day international (ODI)** matches as follows:

```
UPDATE player_batting_averages SET averages = averages + {'number_of_
sixes': 160, 'number_of_fours': 713} WHERE player_id = 9b02528d-75af-
41d9-866e-75d189f57118 AND match_type = 'ODIs'
```

Let's suppose a player has played one test match and scored 50 runs. We could update his statistics as follows:

```
UPDATE player_batting_averages SET averages['Matches'] = 99, averages
['Runs'] = 7656 WHERE player_id = 9b02528d-75af-41d9-866e-75d189f57118
AND match_type = 'Tests'
```

We can also delete a specific record using the key subscript as follows:

```
DELETE averages['number_of_fours'], averages['number_of_sixes'] FROM
player_batting_averages WHERE  player_id = 9b02528d-75af-41d9-866e-
75d189f57118 AND match_type = 'ODIs'
```

UDTs

Cassandra 2.1 and above gives us the flexibility to create our own custom data types, called **User Defined Types** (**UDTs**). This helps us to **denormalize** by putting related data in a single column family. Let's suppose we need to have user ratings for each type of car search in our car database. A rating displays the rating scale, actual rating, and total number of votes. One way to do this could be to create a UDT called ratings and that comprises of these three parameters; then each column family could use this UDT. We can create this UDT as follows:

1. Set up the UDT to have the attributes of native types, collection types, or another UDT type:

```
CREATE TYPE ratings ( scale decimal, rating decimal, total_
votesbigint )
```

 Once a type is created, we can add or rename a field or change the field type, but we cannot delete fields.

2. Now, let's create a column family that displays rating and price information about specific cars searchable by brand and model. The `frozen` keyword with angle brackets is used to define a column as UDT:

```
CREATE TABLE cars_ratings_by_brand( brand text, model text,
price_range text, user_rating frozen<ratings>, PRIMARY KEY
((brand,model)) )
```

3. Now, let's populate this column family with some data:

```
INSERT INTO cars_ratings_by_brand (brand, model,price_range, user_
rating ) VALUES ( 'Audi', 'Q7', '64.4L-79.7L', {scale: 10, rating:
9, total_votes: 10000})
```

UDTs cannot be partly updated; for example, if we only want to update `total_votes` to `11000` and `rating` to `9.2`, we will have to write `scale` to `10` as well.

```
UPDATE cars_ratings_by_brand SET user_rating = { rating: 9.2,
scale: 10, total_votes: 11000} WHERE brand = 'Audi' and model =
'Q7'
```

4. If we omit any attribute, it'll be treated as `null`, for example, if we omit `scale` then it'll be set to null:

```
UPDATE cars_ratings_by_brand SET user_rating = { rating: 9.2,
total_votes: 11000} WHERE brand = 'Audi' and model = 'Q7'
// Output of this will be
SELECT * FROM cars_ratings_by_brand ;
brand | model | price_range | user_rating
-------+-------+-------------+-----------------------------------
------------
  Audi |   Q7 | 64.4L-79.7L | {rating: 9.2, scale: null, total_
votes: 11000}
However we can read selective attributes of a UDT.
SELECT user_rating.rating FROM cars_ratings_by_brand WHERE brand =
'Audi' AND model = 'Q7';
user_rating.rating
--------------------
              9.2
```

Behind the hood, all other attributes of the `rating` column are also read but not displayed.

Since UDTs store complete data in a single column and are written entirely as well as read entirely behind the hood, we should not use them to store very large types.

It's not advisable to use UDTs as primary key columns. However, it is possible to use them as any column.

Secondary indexes

Secondary indexes are indexes on columns that are not part of a primary key. Secondary indexes allow efficient querying on non-primary key columns. This could be the case in some scenarios, for example, the column family for cars:

```
CREATE TABLE cars (
brand text,
```

```
model text,
variant text,
body_type text,
colors set<text>,
mileage decimal,
    PRIMARY KEY (brand, model), variant)
)
```

We might want to be able to search for cars of a specific body type, for example all cars with the `hatchback` body type. In order to achieve this, we could create a secondary index on the `body_type` column as follows:

```
CREATE INDEX cars_body_type ON cars(body_type)
```

Now, we could search for all hatchback cars of all brands, as follows:

```
SELECT * FROM cars WHERE body_type = 'hatchback';

brand  | model | variant                      | body_type | colors
| mileage
-------+-------+------------------------------+-----------+----------
------------------------+---------
Maruti | Swift |                          ZDI | hatchback |
{'Pearl White', 'Red Pearl'} |    18.4
Maruti | Swift |                          ZXI | hatchback |
{'Pearl White', 'Red Pearl'} |    14.4
   Audi |    Q7 |             3.0 TDI QUATTRO | hatchback | {'Apple
Green', 'Titanium Black'} |    13.4
   Audi |    Q7 | 3.0 TDI QUATTRO PREMIUM PLUS | hatchback | {'Apple
Green', 'Titanium Black'} |    13.4
```

 The index name should be unique within a keyspace.

 Indexes should not be created on columns that have unique values for most of the rows. For example, in the preceding `cars` column family, the `body_type` column could be created as an index as this column has low cardinality. If we require efficient queries on high cardinality columns we should consider performing **Denormalization** on such column family by creating another column family with such columns as part of Primary Key instead of creating Secondary Indexes.

If columns get updated or deleted frequently, we should not use indexes.

Secondary indexes are updated asynchronously and are distributed among the nodes in the cluster. A node has indexes only for the data it holds. Since indexes are distributed, consistency level rules apply for them as well.

If there are multiple secondary indexes in a WHERE clause, Cassandra will perform the query first on an index that has lesser results and then on the next and so on.

Secondary indexes cannot be created on counter columns and static columns.

Allowing filtering

Cassandra, by default, only allows those queries which don't require any server-side filtering. Cassandra does this to avoid performance hits that might be caused due to these queries. Let's take the example of the employee table, which stores employee salary details department-wise:

```
CREATE TABLE employee ( emp_id text PRIMARY KEY, first_name text,
last_name text, department text,  salary int )
CREATE INDEX emp_salary ON employee(salary)
CREATE INDEX emp_department ON employee(department)
```

Now, if you want to get the details of all the employees in the sales department with a salary of more than 100000, you might want to run a query as follows:

```
SELECT first_name, last_nameFROM employee WHERE department = 'sales'
AND salary > 100000 //Won't be allowed by cassandra
```

But this query will not be allowed by Cassandra as, in this case, even if there are very few employees who match this criterion, Cassandra will have to filter each row of the sales department to check if it's greater than 100000. But if most the employees match this criterion, then this filtering cost would still be justifiable. So we might want to run this query. We can run such a query by explicitly asking Cassandra to allow filtering, as follows:

```
SELECT first_name, last_nameFROM employee WHERE department = 'sales'
AND salary > 100000 ALLOW FILTERING
```

Allowing filtering should be used with care.

TTL

Sometimes we may want to expire or delete some data after a certain amount of time has elapsed. For example, in a column family of a user's status updates, we don't want to keep status updates of users for more than 100 days. One way of doing this is to create a monitoring job to keep track of such things and then delete such data. However, in Cassandra, these things can be taken care of by the database itself. This means a default **TTL**(**time to live**) operation could be specified for all the data of a column family as well as per `INSERT` or `DELETE` operation. TTL defines a time duration after which Cassandra will start removal process of the data. TTL precision is in seconds. Behind the hood, when a piece of data is removed, a tombstone is put onto it. Later on, tombstones are cleared during garbage collection of the normal compaction process after a period of time specified by the `gc_grace_seconds` configuration option.

 Tombstone age is calculated at each node of a cluster locally, so if a node dies for longer than the duration specified by `gc_grace_seconds`, that node should be considered dead and should be replaced by a new node.

For example, to expire the status updates of users after 100 days in a column family of `status_updates_by_user`, we could define a table as follows:

```
CREATE TABLE status_updates_by_user ( userid text, updated_on
timestamp, status text, PRIMARY KEY (userid, updated_on)) WITH
default_time_to_live = 8640000
```

Now, let's insert some data into it with a time gap:

```
INSERT INTO status_updates_by_user (userid, updated_on , status )
VALUES ( 'usera' , '2015-01-10 12:01:00' , 'Hello World')
INSERT INTO status_updates_by_user (userid, updated_on , status )
VALUES ( 'usera' , '2015-01-10 12:10:00' , 'Howe did people know what
roads to take before google maps was made')
INSERT INTO status_updates_by_user (userid, updated_on , status )
VALUES ( 'usera' , '2015-01-10 12:11:00' , 'saw the dumbest elevator
today, it had a button for the floor I was already on')
// INSERT using TTL
INSERT INTO status_updates_by_user (userid, updated_on , status )
VALUES ( 'usera' , '2015-01-10 10:10:00' , 'Short lived message')
USING TTL 40
```

We can check the time left or the current TTL for each, as follows:

```
SELECT userid, updated_on, status, TTL(status) FROM status_updates_by_
user ;

userid | updated_on                   | status
| ttl(status)
--------+-----------------------------+-----------------------------------
---------------------------------------------------+-------------
usera | 2015-01-10 10:10:00+0530 |
Short lived message |          38
usera | 2015-01-10 12:01:00+0530 |
Hello World |       8638681
usera | 2015-01-10 12:10:00+0530 |            Howe did people know
what roads to take before google maps was made |       8639400
usera | 2015-01-10 12:11:00+0530 | saw the dumbest elevator today, it
had a button for the floor I was already on |       8639417
```

For the very first row, the TTL is only 38 seconds as, while inserting, we specified its TTL as 40 seconds. However, the rest of the rows are inserted with a default TTL of `8640000`. The TTL displayed is less as we checked it after some time.

Similarly, the UPDATE operation can also be done by using TTL.

Conditional querying

We can do conditional querying in Cassandra using the WHERE clause. These conditions can be made using primary key and/or secondary indexed columns.

Conditions on a partition key

Only equality or IN relations are allowed on the queries based on the partition key. Also, IN relations are only allowed on the last part of the partition key. A complete partition key is required in query condition. For example, in the `cars_ratings_by_ table` column family, only the following queries are allowed:

```
SELECT * FROM cars_ratings_by_brand WHERE brand = 'Audi' and model =
'Q7'
SELECT * FROM cars_ratings_by_brand WHERE brand = 'Audi' and model =
'Q7'
SELECT * FROM cars_ratings_by_brand WHERE brand = 'Maruti' AND model
IN ('Q7', 'Swift')
```

The following queries are invalid:

```
SELECT * FROM cars_by_brand WHERE brand IN ('Audi', 'Maruti') AND
model IN ('Q7', 'Swift') // Used IN in first part of partition key
SELECT * FROM cars_by_brand WHeRE brand = 'Maruti' // Incomplete
partition key
```

 A token function could be used to query range searches on a partition key.

Conditions on a partition key and clustering columns

We can query a partition key using one or more clustering columns. However, if not all the clustering columns are being used, then only those clustering columns are allowed in a query which will fetch contiguous rows for that partition key. Consider the following column family, which stores sales information about retail stores at different locations for a retail chain:

```
CREATE TABLE retailstore (city text, location text, sales_info_date
timestamp, total_sales int, PRIMARY KEY (city, location, sales_info_
date))
```

The following queries are valid on this column family:

```
SELECT * FROM retailstore WHERE city = 'gurgaon' AND location = 'sec-
10'
SELECT * FROM retailstore WHERE city = 'gurgaon' AND location = 'sec-
10' AND sales_info_date > '2014-02-01'
SELECT * FROM retailstore WHERE city = 'gurgaon' AND location = 'sec-
14' AND sales_info_date > '2014-02-01' AND sales_info_date < '2015-01-
01'
SELECT * FROM retailstore WHERE city = 'gurgaon' AND location = 'sec-
14' AND sales_info_date = '2014-02-10'
```

However, the following queries, which try to fetch noncontiguous logical rows are not valid, as clustering columns are mentioned out of order. We could use column sales_info_date only when we're also using location column in our query because while creating column family retailstore, location column was defined first and then sales_info_date was defined:

```
SELECT * FROM retailstore WHERE city = 'gurgaon' AND sales_info_date =
'2013-02-10'
SELECT * FROM retailstore WHERE city = 'gurgaon' AND sales_info_date >
'2013-02-10'
```

Sorting query results

The ORDER BY clause lets us sort query results in either ascending or descending order. Currently, the ORDER BY clause supports the ordering of columns in the same order mentioned in the primary key:

```
SELECT * FROM retailstore WHERE city = 'gurgaon' ORDER BY location
DESC, sales_info_date ASC // Invalid
SELECT * FROM retailstore WHERE city = 'gurgaon' ORDER BY location
DESC, sales_info_date DESC // Valid
SELECT * FROM retailstore WHERE city = 'gurgaon' ORDER BY location ,
sales_info_date // Valid
SELECT * FROM retailstore WHERE city = 'gurgaon' ORDER BY  sales_info_
date // Invalid
SELECT * FROM retailstore WHERE city = 'gurgaon' ORDER BY  location //
valid
```

The LIMIT option can be used to limit the number of rows returned.

Write operations

In Cassandra, both UPDATE and INSERT statements are write operations, which means that these operation don't do any reading before writing. This implies that, if we're executing an UPDATE operation on a primary key and the row for that primary key doesn't exist, UPDATE will insert a new row.

Similarly, if we're performing an INSERT operation and the row mentioned in the INSERT operation identified by the primary key already exists in the database, that row will be overwritten by our INSERT operation.

This is why we call them UPSERT operations as well.

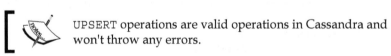 UPSERT operations are valid operations in Cassandra and won't throw any errors.

Lightweight transactions

Sometimes, it could be the case that we are running two operations in parallel but want them to be executed in a serial manner, one after another. For example, if two users are registering them to the system with the same user ID at the same point in time or a user account is being updated by two different means at the same time. These tasks should run in serial in order to guarantee that the data is in the correct state for both operations; otherwise, one operation might overwrite the other's record and the first one will never know. Serialization of such task becomes hard if there are multiple nodes serving requests. In traditional database systems it was achieved by routing such requests only to one node called master node which then does serialization, however this way the cluster becomes partially functional if master node is down. In a master-less database like Cassandra it was hard to achieve as read write could go to any node. **Lightweight Transaction (LWT)** in Cassandra version 2.0 and above solves such problems. LWT introduced the IF clause in INSERT and UPDATE statements which serializes write operations for a given primary key.

The LWT query for user account creation would be as follows. Suppose two users try to create an account with the name nitinp, only one will succeed:

```
INSERT INTO users (userid, firstname , lastname , primary_phone ,
alternate_phone, address ) VALUES ( 'nitinp', 'nitin', 'padalia',
'123456', '654321', 'sec-10') IF NOT EXISTS;


 [applied]
-----------
     True
// Second query will fail with applied as false
INSERT INTO users (userid, firstname , lastname , primary_phone ,
alternate_phone, address ) VALUES ( 'nitinp', 'nitin', 'pandey',
'142536', '635241', 'sec-18') IF NOT EXISTS ;


[applied] | userid | address | alternate_phone | firstname | lastname
| primary_phone
-----------+--------+---------+-----------------+-----------+---------
--+---------------
    False | nitinp |  sec-10 |          654321 |     nitin | padalia
|       123456
```

Now suppose, after some time, the user's phone numbers and address information got changed and they want to update it. The user goes to update his phone numbers and address using his cell phone:

```
UPDATE users SET primary_phone = '112233', alternate_phone = '554422',
address = 'sec-15' WHERE userid = 'nitinp' IF primary_phone = '123456'
AND alternate_phone = '65432
1' AND address = 'sec-10';

 [applied]
-----------
      True
```

However, at the same time, his wife (who is only aware of the address change but not the phone number change) is updating account information using her cell phone:

```
UPDATE users SET primary_phone = '123456', alternate_phone = '654321',
address = 'sec-15' WHERE userid = 'nitinp' IF  primary_phone =
'123456' AND alternate_phone = '65432' AND address = 'sec-10';

 [applied] | primary_phone | alternate_phone | address
-----------+---------------+-----------------+---------
     False |        112233 |          554422 | sec-15
```

We can see, using a LWT query, the returned failure for her update; if this had not happened, she would have overwritten the changes made by her husband.

These transactions will only lock partitions with the user ID `nitinp`, so other users with different user IDs won't be affected by this.

We should read such records with consistency level SERIAL since serial consistency commits any uncommitted changes during read operations. We'll be discussing more about consistency levels in the next chapter.

Batch statements

Cassandra supports the execution of multiple INSERT / UPDATE / DELETE operations in a batch. This way, client programs can save the time it takes to send queries multiple times to the server. In versions above 1.2, default batch statements are atomic. This means either all the statements of a batch will be completed or none will. Statements inside a batch are not isolated. So, if a batch is being executed and has completed some of the statements inside it, then a parallel running client can read those changes. However, updates belonging to a partition key are isolated:

```
BEGIN BATCH
```

```
INSERT INTO cars (brand, model, variant , body_type, colors, mileage)
VALUES ( 'Audi', 'Q1', '3.0 TDI QUATTRO', 'Sedan', {'Apple Green',
'Titanium Black'},
14.2);
UPDATE cars SET body_type = 'Sedan' WHERE brand='Audi' AND model ='Q7'
AND variant = '3.0 TDI QUATTRO PREMIUM PLUS';
APPLY BATCH;
```

Atomicity comes at some performance cost. To avoid it, UNLOGGED batches could be used. These batches will be atomic at partition key level:

```
BEGIN UNLOGGED BATCH
INSERT INTO cars (brand, model, variant , body_type, colors, mileage)
VALUES ( 'Audi', 'Q1', '3.0 TDI QUATTRO', 'Sedan', {'Apple Green',
'Titanium Black'},
14.2);
UPDATE cars SET body_type = 'Sedan' WHERE brand='Audi' AND model ='Q7'
AND variant = '3.0 TDI QUATTRO PREMIUM PLUS';
APPLY BATCH;
```

Batches can contain only INSERT, UPDATE, or DELETE statements.

BEGIN COUNTER BATCH should be used for counter batched operations.

The timestamp statement could be used with DML statements within a batch or it could be used at batch level. If it is used at batch level, it must not be used with a DML statement inside it.

Summary

Cassandra keyspaces and column families are different from regular SQL databases and tables. A partition key row lies completely on a node, and it can have multiple logical rows uniquely identified by the primary key. A column family with one or more clustering columns in its primary key can have multiple logical rows per partition, so these column families are called wide rows. Rows per partition key are sorted based on the clustering columns. While reading records we can only search by either partition key or clustering columns. Secondary index columns can also be used to filter search data. Cassandra, by default, prevents running those queries that involve filtering. LWTs can help to serialize concurrent operations at some performance cost. Multiple related DML statements can be grouped together by BATCH statements. Default batch statements are atomic and are costlier in terms of performance. The UNLOGGED batches could be used if atomicity isn't required and performance is more important.

4
Read and Write – Behind the Scenes

We now know how we can read or write our data to Cassandra using **CQL**. But we haven't discussed what Cassandra actually does whenever we fire a read or write query. In this chapter, we'll discuss what is being done by Cassandra behind the scenes during our read or write requests. We'll see what all caching features does Cassandra provides are, and you'll see how they are applied by Cassandra so that we can enable them according to our needs. We'll also discuss write operations and a compaction process run to save disk space occupied by redundant data in various `SSTable` formed due to multiple flush operations over time. There are three compaction strategies; if used wisely, an appropriate compaction could make our search operation faster.

Write operations

During a write request by a client, the coordinator node finds the replicas for the partition key based on the partitioner being used. It then sends the write request to all the nodes that are owners of that partition key range. Coordinator nodes return write success to the client as soon as many number of nodes return write success based on the consistency requirement of the write operation. Let's assume that three nodes are replica nodes for a write operation and the write operation is being done at `QUORUM` consistency; whenever two out of three nodes return success for the write operation, the coordinator node acknowledges a write operation success to the client. We'll learn more about consistency in the next sections.

On a node, a write request is first written to a file called `CommitLog`, and then in a memory data structure called a `Memtable`. Whenever Memtables are full, they are flushed to disk in files called `SSTable`. A replica node acknowledges a write operation success as soon as it is written in the `CommitLog` and `Memtable`.

CommitLog

The `CommitLog` file is used to make the write durable. In the event that the node dies, `CommitLog` is replayed to recover the data. `Commitlog` is written in append only mode, so if `CommitLog` has its own disk assigned in `Cassandra.yaml`, write operations would be pretty fast, as disks would be written only in append mode and disk head movement would be at least causing less time doing seek.

The `CommitLog` file is written to the disk in two modes: periodic and batch. Periodic mode is the default synching mode. We can set our preferred mode in `Cassandra.yaml` using the `commitlog_sync` configuration option. In periodic mode, acknowledgement to write operations is returned immediately and data is synched to the disk in the time specified by `commitlog_sync_period_in_ms`, in milliseconds, which is configurable in `Cassandra.yaml` file.

Batch mode does not acknowledge write operations until it is written to the disk. In this mode, all write operations that occur during the time window determined by the configuration option `commitlog_sync_batch_window_in_ms` in the `Cassandra.yaml` file are grouped. In the preceding figure, you can see the write flow for batch operations, depicted by **1', 2', 3', 4'** and **5'**. Here, the client write is not acknowledged before `fsyncing` writes to `CommitLog` in disk.

> In Batch mode write ACK are sent after data fsyncing is done to disk. This implies that batch mode's efficiency is directly affected by time taken by commit log write to disk operation hence it's advised that we've a separate disk for commit logs so that commit log writes don't contend with other write operations.

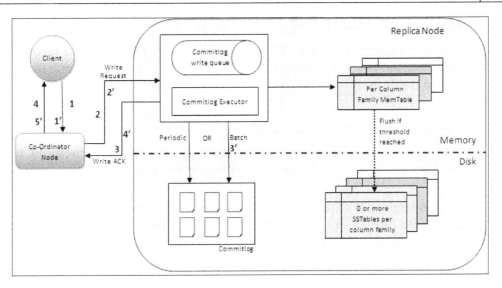

Data is written into `CommitLog` file segments, which are recycled once data for that column family is flushed to the disk in the form of a `SSTable` from the `Memtable`. For each column family, a marker is kept to keep track of where in `CommitLog` the last write operation was done for that column family. Once data from the `Memtable` is flushed to disk for that column family, the marker is advanced, and segments before that marker are marked as clean and can be recycled. The configuration option `commitlog_segment_size_in_mb` determines a segment size, whereas `commitlog_total_space_in_mb` specifies the total space allocated to `CommitLog`. If `CommitLog` space use goes above this value, the `Memtable` with data in the oldest `CommitLog` segment will be flushed to disk, and markers in that segment will be cleaned.

The `CommitLog` location is defined by the `Cassandra.yaml` configuration option `commitlog_directory`. If it is not set, it'll be saved in `$CASSANDRA_HOME/data/commitlog`.

The following snapshot shows a `CommitLog` section with various segment files:

```
# cd /opt/Cassandra/data/commitlog
# ls
CommitLog-4-1428560363142.log   CommitLog-4-1428560363147.log   CommitLog-4-1428560363152.log
CommitLog-4-1428560363157.log   CommitLog-4-1428560363162.log   CommitLog-4-1428560363167.log
CommitLog-4-1428560363143.log   CommitLog-4-1428560363148.log   CommitLog-4-1428560363153.log
CommitLog-4-1428560363158.log   CommitLog-4-1428560363163.log   CommitLog-4-1428560363168.log
CommitLog-4-1428560363144.log   CommitLog-4-1428560363149.log   CommitLog-4-1428560363154.log
CommitLog-4-1428560363159.log   CommitLog-4-1428560363164.log   CommitLog-4-1428560363169.log
CommitLog-4-1428560363145.log   CommitLog-4-1428560363150.log   CommitLog-4-1428560363155.log
CommitLog-4-1428560363160.log   CommitLog-4-1428560363165.log   CommitLog-4-1428560363170.log
CommitLog-4-1428560363146.log   CommitLog-4-1428560363151.log   CommitLog-4-1428560363156.log
CommitLog-4-1428560363161.log   CommitLog-4-1428560363166.log   CommitLog-4-1428560363171.log
```

Anatomy of Memtable

The Memtable is an in-memory data structure used by Cassandra to make read and write requests faster. Each column family has one Memtable associated with it. A Memtable can reside in memory until one of the following:

1. The space used by the commitlog file exceeds the configured threshold, as discussed in the Commitlog section.

2. The total space used by all Memtables exceeds a configurable threshold. In such a scenario, Cassandra stops accepting write operations until a flush is completed. It also triggers a flush operation.

3. A manual flush is requested by using the nodetool flush command. This command flushes all Memtables to disk from memory. This is generally done before restarting a node so that commitLog replay time can be reduced when nodes come back again.

Upon reaching the threshold, Memtables are flushed to disk in the form of the SSTable. By default, Memtables are stored on-heap; however, we can change their storage to off-heap using the configuration option memtable_allocation_type in Cassandra.yaml.

SSTable explained

Flushed in-memory Memtables are stored in immutable disk files called SSTable. Here, immutable means that for every flush operation of a Memtable of a column family, a different SSTable is formed. So, if 10 flush operations have occurred for a column family, 10 different SSTable files will be created by each flush operation. Thus, each column family could have 0 or more SSTable associated with it.

When a SSTable is written, Cassandra maintains the following three structures for them:

1. The PartitionIndex file: This file is stored on disk along with the SSTable and keeps track of all partition keys in that SSTable This file also helps to find the offset of the start of the data for that partition key in the SSTable file.

2. PartitionIndexSummary: This is an in-memory structure that keeps samples from the PartitionIndex file. By default, every 128th entry from the PartitionIndex file is sampled into PartitionIndexSummary for frequently used column families. It can be controlled using table configuration options min_index_interval and max_index_interval. We discussed these configuration options in the previous chapter. Cassandra uses these samples to find the location of partition key entries in PartitionIndex using binary search.

3. `BloomFilter`: Since a column family could have multiple `SSTable` associated with it due to multiple flush operations, data for a partition key could be spread among multiple `SSTable`. So, to find out which `SSTable` should be consulted to get the data, Cassandra employs a probabilistic data structure called `BloomFilter`. Every `SSTable` has one `BloomFilter` data structure associated with it. `BloomFilter` tells us whether given partition key data exists in a given `SSTable` or not. If `BloomFilter` says the data is not there, the `SSTable` will certainly not have that data in it. On the other hand, if it says it does, then it might or might not be there. Accuracy of `BloomFilter` is configurable and discussed in detail in *Chapter 6, Monitoring and Tuning a Cassandra Cluster*, however more accurate a bloom filter is the more space it'll occupy.

Let's take an example of a write operation. Assume we've a column family with four columns in it and the sampling index interval for the column family is two. We're taking a lower index interval to keep our example simple. We're showing used `CommitLog` segments in grey and free ones in white.

Suppose we've done six write operations, with partition keys K1, K2, K3, K4, K5, and K6. The respective columns for each partition are shown in following figure. These write operations caused to write `CommitLog` segment as - 1, shown in grey in the following figure. Also the `Memtable` is populated for that:

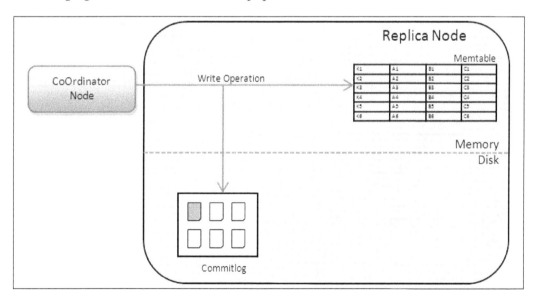

Read and Write – Behind the Scenes

Now suppose that, after some time, the `Memtable` threshold is hit and the `Memtable` is flushed to the disk, forming a `SSTable` and its respective `PartitionIndex`, `IndexSummary`, and `BloomFilter` data structure, as shown in the following figure. This causes `CommitLog` segment -1 to get recycled. `IndexSummary` has three entries, as our sampling interval is configured as two for the column family, as shown in the following figure:

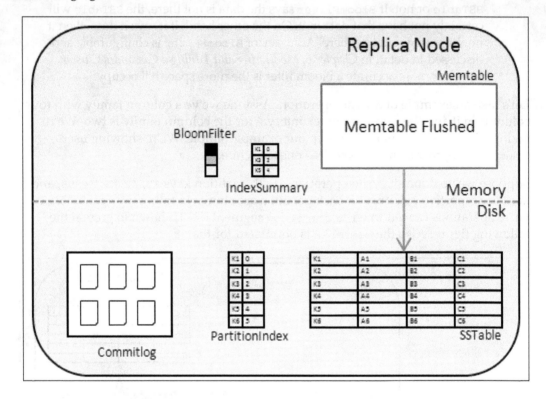

We performed a write operation on that column family once again, inserted one new row with key K7, and updated all columns of key K1. As a result, a `CommitLog` will be written and its `Memtable` will be populated, as shown in the following figure. Note that the `SSTable` is still populated as `Memtable` is still in memory:

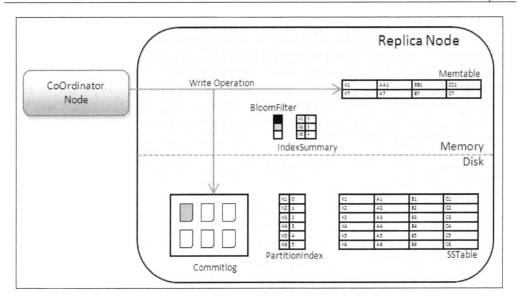

After a while, this `Memtable` also gets flushed to disk, and since `SSTable` are immutable by nature, this operation creates a new file (`SSTable-2`) with new updates. The respective `PartitionIndex`, `IndexSummary`, and `BloomFilter` data structure are created for this new `SSTable`:

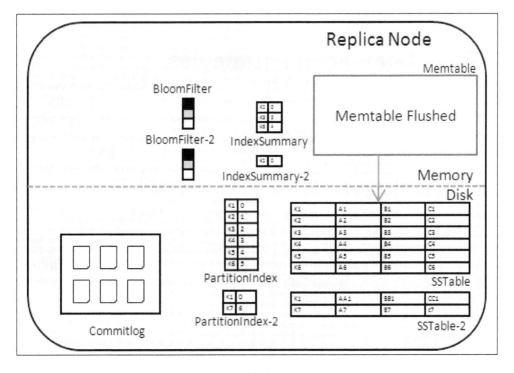

You can find the SSTable at a location defined by the Cassandra.yaml configuration option data_file_directories. If it is not set, you can find the SSTable and PartitionIndex files for all column families at a location defined by $CASSANDRA_HOME/data/data/<keyspace-name>/<column-famil-name-*>/. For example, if the Cassandra installation directory is /opt/Cassandra, the keyspace name is userdb, and the column family is user_status_updates, then the SSTable location will be /opt/Cassandra/data/data/userdb/user_status_updates-*, as shown in the following code snippet:

```
# cd /opt/Cassandra/data/data/userdb
# ls
user_status_updates-bf316g30ebdf11e4a51b811a5d39e8fc
```

You can see the SSTable and the PartitionIndex file inside the column family directory, as shown here highlighted as grey Data.db is SSTable and Index.db is PartitionIndex file:

```
# cd user_status_updates-bf316g30ebdf11e4a51b811a5d39e8fc/
# ls
userdb-user_status_updates-ka-1-CompressionInfo.db  userdb-user_
status_updates-ka-1-Digest.sha1  userdb-user_status_updates-ka-1-
Index.db         userdb-user_status_updates-ka-1-Summary.db
userdb-user_status_updates-ka-1-Data.db               userdb-user_
status_updates-ka-1-Filter.db     userdb-user_status_updates-ka-1-
Statistics.db  userdb-user_status_updates-ka-1-TOC.txt
```

SSTable Compaction strategies

As the column family grows with time, there could be multiple SSTable associated with it. To fulfil a read operation, Cassandra might therefore have to consult multiple SSTable. This means multiple disk I/Os, and consequently slower read operations. To improve this scenario, Cassandra employs a compaction process, which merges multiple SSTable into one new SSTable, enabling lesser disk I/O for a search operation in a column family. This also frees up disk space occupied by old data or deleted data spread across multiple SSTable formed over time.

Compaction is triggered automatically by Cassandra based on the compaction strategy set for each column family. This type of compaction is called minor compaction. However, we can also run compaction manually using the nodetool command. This manual compaction merges all SSTable of a column family into a single new one. However, we typically would not be running a major compaction.

Compaction is configurable for each column family, and the compaction table property is used for this. We can configure one from the three different compaction strategies available for a column family. Strategies should be chosen based on the data access pattern for data stored in the column family at hand.

Size-tiered compaction

Size-tiered compaction is the default compaction strategy set for a column family if we don't specify a strategy explicitly. This compaction strategy starts merging multiple SSTable into one SSTable when the SSTable of similar size formed for a column family are equal to or more than a configured default (the default is four). This means that if by default four SSTable of similar size are formed for a column family, Cassandra will merge them into a new SSTable of a bigger size. The minimum number of SSTable required to start a minor compaction can be configured using the configuration option of the column family property called min_threshold. By default, Cassandra will form a compaction bucket of most 32 SSTable, which is configurable from the table property max_threshold. Cassandra uses the table configuration options bucket_low and bucket_high to decide which SSTable are similar in size, and form a compaction bucket. The default values are 0.5 and 1.5, respectively, which means it'll group all SSTable in a bucket if their sizes differ by 50 percent from their average size. There is one more table configuration option, called min_sstable_size, which puts all SSTable below this size in the same compaction bucket. Its default value is 50 MB, so all SSTable smaller than 50 MB will be put in the same compaction bucket.

So, if we've eight SSTable, sized 1, 75, 10, 115, 25, 5, 85, and 125 MB, one bucket will be of all SSTable smaller than 50 MB, that is **[1,10,25,5]** and the second would be **[75,85,115,125]**.

The following figure shows how two compaction runs merged eight SSTable into two SSTable. Note that the second compaction run didn't pick the very first SSTable because it did not fall in the bucket_low and bucket_high range:

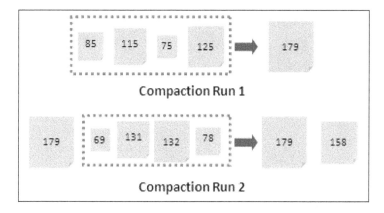

Leveled compaction

In the leveled compaction strategy, the SSTable size is kept small - 160 MB by default. SSTable are grouped into different levels, L0, L1, L2, and so on. Each level has a fixed size and is 10x bigger than the previous level. In SizeTiered compaction, a row can be spread over multiple SSTable if frequent updates are happening on that row. If that is the case, the read will be slower for those rows. This level guarantees that, within a level, rows will not be duplicated in different SSTable. Also, 90 percent of the time a read will be satisfied by a single SSTable. Effectively, fewer disk I/Os are required when searching for a row as compared to SizeTiered compaction.

A newly created SSTable is grouped in L0 and immediately compacted to SSTable in level L1, increasing the size of the L1 group. The preceding figure shows this behavior. Lets have a look th the following figure:

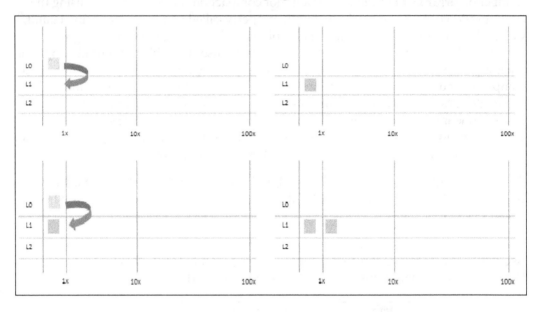

When the L1 size limit is reached, extra `SSTable` are grouped into the next level, L2. Now onwards, each `SSTable` added to L1 will be compacted with the `SSTable` in L2. The same process will be followed for the next levels. This is depicted in the preceding figure. Let's have a look at the following figure:

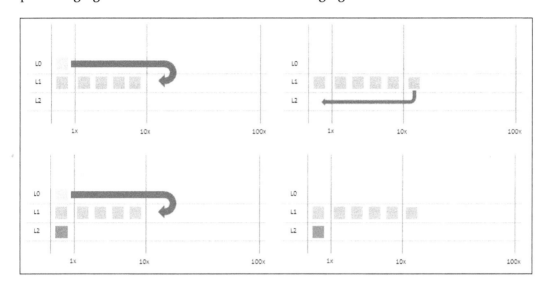

LeveledTiered compaction reduces disk seeks in a read operation for a partition key in `SSTable` by reducing the number of `SSTable` that have the same record. However, in order to do that, this compaction process itself does a lot of I/O operations.

DateTiered compaction

Cassandra release 2.0.11 and 2.1.1 onwards introduced a new compaction strategy designed for time series data. The `DateTiered` compaction strategy does compaction based on the age of the `SSTable`. It puts `SSTable` of different ages into different time windows: if there is more than one `SSTable` in a time window, they are nominated for compaction. A new time window is created in unit time (in seconds) specified by `base_time_seconds`; this is 3600 by default. So by default, after every one hour, a new time window is created. When the total number of same-size time windows reaches the value set for `max_threshold`, the configuration options are merged to form a bigger time window. The `Max_threshold` is set to 4 by default, so after four time windows are created, and as soon as fifth time window is formed, the previous four will merge into a single window. The sizes of older time windows keep growing, as do the sizes of the `SSTable` they contain. When a `SSTable` age is more than that specified by `max_sstable_age_days`, the compaction for the `SSTable` is stopped. The default value of `max_sstable_age_days` is 365:

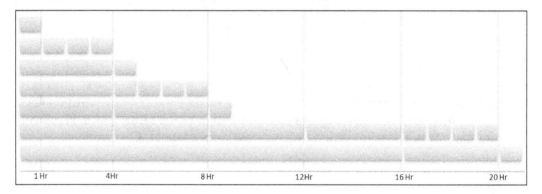

In the preceding figure, we can see that there was only one time window for the very first hour. After 4 hours, the threshold set by `max_threshold` was reached, and all the time windows merged to form a bigger window four hours in size. After eight hours, the next four merged to form a second four-hour window, and after twenty hours `max_threshold` was reached for window size four hours, so they merged to form a sixteen-hour window.

Suppose that after 20 hours we're running a range query to fetch records of the last four hours. We can see that only two `SSTable` would be consulted; however, this might not be the case with the previous two compaction strategies.

The `SizeTiered` compaction strategy is good for insert-oriented data access patterns as it does fewer I/Os for the compaction process. Also, there would be fewer chances that a row would be laying across multiple SSTables. One of the examples where this strategy could be used is Database of a micro blogging site, where data is inserted most of the times and updated once in a while; for example; most frequent operation are user creation, status updates by users etc. These all are insert operations. However update operations like edit a status or a user profile is done not so frequently.

LeveledCompaction strategy should be chosen for a column family having multiple updates over time so that a row is not spread over multiple `SSTable` This strategy could be chosen for inventory management database of an online store, where inventory details is updated frequently.

`DateTiered` compaction is good for time series data or data which is written at a steady rate. If many `read repairs` are happening in the system for a column family, then its compaction might become less efficient. This strategy is also good at removing tombstones so it would be a best fit when we're collecting time series data and purging old data at some regular time interval. One example could be a consensus database like daily opinion poll by some TV channel on some random subject, where audiences are sending opinions during the day and data of opinion poll of last day is not required.

Read operations

When a client requests data from a coordinator node, the coordinator node sends that request to all replica nodes responsible for owning the data. Replica nodes fetch data and respond to the coordinator node; the coordinator node then compares this data and responds to the client with the most recent data returned by the replicas.

A replica node may return data from a cache called row cache, or it might need to consult the `SSTable` and give merged data from both `Memtable` and `SSTable`.

Reads from row cache

A row cache is an off-heap cache that caches frequently accessed rows. It is configured at column family level and is optional. It caches complete or partial partition rows. In previous versions of Cassandra, it used to store complete the partition key row; however, in the 2.1 release, we can also configure how many clustering rows for a partition key should be cached. For example, the following CREATE statement will cache the latest 10 status updates from a user:

```
CREATE TABLE user_status_updates (
useridtext,
status_update_time timestamp,
status_msg text,
PRIMARY KEY (userid, status_update_time)
) WITH CLUSTERING ORDER BY (status_update_time DESC )
AND caching = {'keys': 'ALL', 'rows_per_partition': 10};
```

As rows are cached, we can also configure the caching of frequently-accessed partition keys. These keys are cached in KeyCache.

In the preceding CREATE statement, we mentioned caching option keys to ALL, which means both key caching and row caching is enabled for this column family. Other options could be as follows:

- ROWS_ONLY: Only the row cache will be enabled.
- KEYS_ONLY: Only the key cache will be enabled. Default setting.
- NONE: Caching will be disabled.
- ALL: Both the key cache and the row cache will be enabled.

A row gets populated in row caches whenever it is read for the first time, so the first read of a row from a column family that has the row cache enabled will consult Memtable and SSTable. However, subsequent reads will be served by the row cache, thus saving disk seeks. A write/update over a row invalidates the row cache. Since row caches are maintained in RAM, these should not be used with very large or frequently-updated rows. Let's have a look at the following figure:

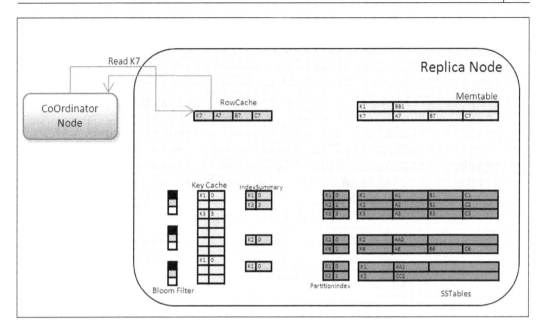

The preceding figure shows that when a read request for partition key **K7** reaches a replica node and the row cache is enabled for the column family. Since the row is cached in RowCache, the request result is returned from the row cache immediately without consulting the Memtable and SSTables.

Read operations for row cache miss

If a column family has no row cache configured or a row cache is not populated yet, it'll be served by the SSTable and Memtables of that column family. It's possible that there will be more than one SSTable for a column family being searched, and the row being searched might be in none of them or in one or more of them. So, to determine whether the row being searched is in a SSTable is or not, Cassandra consults the BloomFilter data structure for each SSTable. As discussed earlier, BloomFilter can filter out all SSTable that certainly don't have that data. After that, Cassandra looks in PartitionKeyCache for the partition key being searched. If KeyCache has the entry, it gets the offset of that partition in the SSTable from there; if KeyCache is missed, it goes to the PartitionIndexSummary data structure to find the location of that row's partition key in the PartitionIndex file. The PartitionIndex file indicates the offset of that partition key in the SSTable. After knowing the offset data is read from SSTable. So, this type of read could either hit KeyCache or miss it. Let's take examples of both these scenarios.

Key is in KeyCache

Now suppose a read request comes for partition key **K1**. Since the row with this partition key is not in RowCache, Cassandra will consult all three BloomFilter of the column family. After consultation with BloomFilter, it is found that only two SSTable have entries for partition key **K1**. So, it searches for **K1** in KeyCache, and voila! Key **K1** is found in KeyCache. Now we can skip consultation with IndexSummary and directly find it in both SSTable. SSTable consultation returns result set **AA1, B1**, and **C1**. Now it searches for key **K1** in the Memtable, and it is found that Memtable also has one column update record, **BB1**, for the key. It merges this result with the result set found in the SSTable and returns a final result set [**AA1, BB1, C1**] to the coordinator node. If the row cache is enabled, this result set is added to RowCache, as shown in the preceding figure. Let's have a look at the following figure:

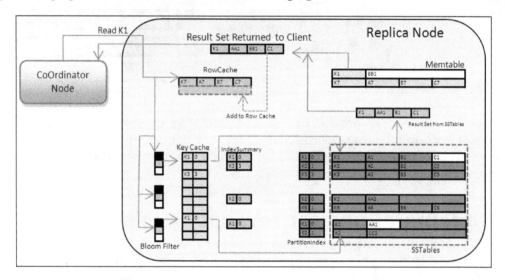

Key search miss both the key cache and the row cache

Now a new read request for partition key **K2** arrives. It isn't found in the row cache, so it goes to BloomFilter, which indicates that the **K2** row is there in all three SSTable. Then it searches the key in KeyCache, but it's not there either. Therefore, Cassandra will have to go through IndexSummary and then PartitionIndex to find the location of the row in the SSTable. Note that this time we did one more disk seek per SSTable. After consultation with all three SSTable, we find that **A2** is updated to **AA2** and **C2** is updated to **CC2**, so the result set is [**AA2, B2, CC2**]. Memtable has no record for key **K2**, so the final result set is [**AA2, B2, CC2**], which is returned to the coordinator node. If the row cache is enabled, this result set is added to RowCache. The preceding figure shows this behavior. Let's have a look at the following figure:

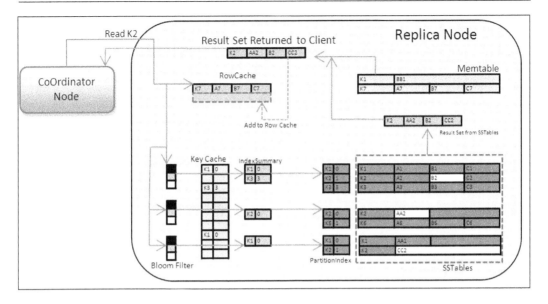

We can use the `nodetool info` command (as shown in the following code snippet) to see if our row caches or key caches are being used, and what their usage per node is:

```
nodetool info
ID                 : 2f9bb0a9-db48-4146-83c9-4ce06bd22259
Gossip active      : true
Thrift active      : true
Native Transport active: true
Load               : 225.66 MB
Generation No      : 1428560369
Uptime (seconds)   : 1470943
Heap Memory (MB)   : 552.50 / 920.00
Data Center        : datacenter1
Rack               : rack1
Exceptions         : 0
Key Cache          : entries 547, size 42.22 KB, capacity 45 MB, 75740
hits, 79424 requests, 0.954 recent hit rate, 14400 save period in
seconds
Row Cache          : entries 0, size 0 bytes, capacity 600 MB, 0 hits, 0
requests, NaN recent hit rate, 3000 save period in seconds
Counter Cache      : entries 0, size 0 bytes, capacity 22 MB, 0 hits, 0
requests, NaN recent hit rate, 7200 save period in seconds
Token              : (invoke with -T/--tokens to see all 256 tokens)
```

We can see in the above trace that 95 percent of all requests hit the key cache. RowCache is not being used at all.

Delete operations

In Cassandra, a delete operation does not delete the requested data immediately. Instead, it puts a marker over the deleted data. This marker is called a tombstone. A tombstone's age is defined by per-column family option gc_grace_seconds. After gc_grace_seconds has passed, Cassandra clears data marked with tombstones, and it clears all tombstones during the compaction of the column family.

> If a node is down for loger than the time specified by gc_grace_ seconds and is recovered, there is a chance that the deleted data will come back. To avoid such scenarios, nodes dead for such a long time should be replaced instead of being added back to the cluster.

Data consistency

Consistency in Cassandra refers to the guarantee that even though a read or write operation in a Cassandra cluster is written to or read from a desired number of nodes, all of them have the same latest data. For example, if we're writing to a Cassandra cluster of five nodes on a column family with a replication factor of 3, we could specify, using consistency, how many nodes should respond to our read or write request in order to guarantee that data returned is the latest and is consistent across all nodes. For example, if the consistency is ONE, the read operation is acknowledged as a success by coordinator node as soon as one node responds3. The consistency level is configurable in Cassandra and can be set per read or write operation.

Read operation

When a read request arrives at a coordinator node, it sends an actual read request to one of closet replica by proximity and digest read request to other nodes as required by the consistency level specified in the read operation. Proximity is determined by snitch configuration. For example, if the read is being operated on data with replication factor 3, and consistency is asked as QUORUM, then an actual read will be sent to the closest replica node, and one digest read request will be sent to another node. If replicas do not respond within a configurable period of time, ReadTimeoutException is raised. If digest of actual read response and digest read response do not match, Cassandra sends a full read request to the node which had been requested the digest read before. Now it matches both the responses and sends the latest data to the client. However, a background read repair is sent to nodes to synchronize their data.

Digest reads

Digest read returns the hash digest of actual data. Digest reads are done to ascertain whether nodes have the same data or not. If digests differ, it means the data is different. Cassandra will send a full read request, compare timestamps, and then return the latest data to the client. However, for old data it triggers a `read repair`.

Read repair

Using read repair, Cassandra fixes any mismatches in data versions in replica nodes for a given partition key. If `read repair` is enabled, digest reads are sent to all replicas during a read request query, and Cassandra compares them and checks whether or not all replicas have the same version of the data. If any replicas have older data, it pushes the most recent version of the data to those nodes with older data. `Read repair` is done in the background and the read is not blocked for completion of the 3 `read repair`. However, for consistency level `ALL`, the read request is blocked until the `read repair` fixes all nodes with older data.

Consistency levels

The following are the consistency levels for read operations:

- `ONE`: The coordinator contacts the closest node by proximity and returns the read result to the client; also, the `read repair` is triggered. If the contacted node has stale data, the same will be returned. However, it can tolerate replica node unavailability better than other levels.

- `TWO`: This is similar to `ONE`, but the read must be acknowledged by two nodes instead of one node.

- `THREE`: This is again similar to `ONE`, but the read must be acknowledged by three nodes in this case.

- `LOCAL_ONE`: This is relevant for multi-datacenter deployments. A read operation using this consistency will return read results by contacting a single replica node in the same datacenter as that of the coordinator node.

- `QUORUM`: The result set is returned to the client as soon as 51 percent (the defined quorum) of the replica nodes have responded to the coordinator node from any datacenter. For example, if the replication factor is 3, the `QUORUM` would be 2.

- `LOCAL_QUORUM`: The result set is returned to the client as soon as 51 percent (the defined quorum) of the replicas of the same datacenter as the coordinator respond to the read request.

- `EACH_QUORUM`: The result set is returned when 51 percent (the defined quorum) of the replicas from all datacenters have responded.

- `ALL`: The result set is not returned unless all replica nodes have responded to the request. If any of them fail, the request is considered as failed. This is useful if high consistency is required, disregarding high availability.

- `SERIAL`: This level should be used to read those columns which were written using lightweight transaction features. This reads the latest data from **Lightweight Transaction (LWT)** and commits any uncommitted transactions. Read success is acknowledged when `QUORUM` replicas read using serial condition.

- `LOCAL_SERIAL`: This is almost the same as `SERIAL`, but is only limited to the local datacenter.

Let's have a look at the following figure:

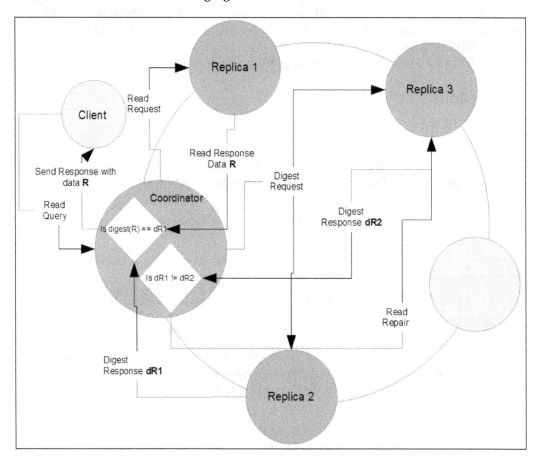

The preceding figure shows a read operation with consistency level QUORUM on a 5-node cluster with replication factor 3. The client sends a request to the coordinator node, which then sends an actual read request to Replica 1, as Replica 1 was closest - that is, it was in the same rack. Also, since the read is of QUORUM level, an additional digest request was sent to a second node, Replica 2, which was the fastest responding replica. After some time, Replica 1 returned with data R and Replica 2 with digest dR1. Here, the digest of read request data from Replica 1 matches the digest response returned by Replica 2, so the coordinator node sends result set R to the client. Since read repair was enabled, a background digest request was sent to Replica 3. Digest response dR1 and digest response dR2 from nodes.

Replica 2 and Replica 3, respectively, didn't match, and it was found that Replica 3 had data with an older timestamp, so a read repair was triggered to Replica 3.

Write operation

A write request is sent to all replica nodes by the coordinator node. If all of them are up and running, eventually it'll be written to all nodes. However, deciding when to consider a write request a success and acknowledge it to the client is determined by the consistency level used during the write operation. For example, if the replication factor is 3 and we're using QUORUM as the consistency during write, as soon as two replica nodes write data to their respective CommitLog and Memtable, the write operation is acknowledged as a success to the client by the coordinator node without waiting for a success to be returned by the third node.

Hinted handoff

This feature enables writing a row to be successful even if all replica nodes owning that row are down. When all replicas are down for a given row key, Cassandra writes a hint to the coordinator node. This hint is played back to replica nodes when they are recovered. Hinted handoff is only applicable for consistency setting ANY, as described in the following subsection.

Consistency levels

The following consistency levels are allowed during a write operation:

- ONE: The write operation is acknowledged as a success when one replica node writes successfully and responds to the coordinator node.

- TWO: This is almost the same as ONE, but the number of nodes that should return a write success is two instead of one.

- THREE: Again, this is almost the same as ONE, but three nodes must acknowledge the write operation as a success instead of one.

- LOCAL_ONE: When at least one node from the local datacenter acknowledges the write operation as success to the coordinator, the coordinator marks it as a success and sends an acknowledgement back to the client.

- QUORUM: When the write operation is succeeded at QUORUM replica nodes, the success is acknowledged to the client.

- LOCAL_QUORUM: The client gets a success response as soon as QUORUM replicas from the local datacenter of the coordinator node respond with a successful write operation.

- EACH_QUORUM: The client has to wait until QUORUM replicas in all datacenters write data in their respective CommitLog and Memtable. When all replicas meeting the quorum finish writing and inform the coordinator node, the coordinator returns write operation success.

- ALL: This is used only for write operations that are expected to be highly consistent, as write operations will be blocked unless all replica nodes respond with a successful write operation.

- ANY: This provides the highest possible availability with Cassandra, but with the lowest consistency. Write response is comparatively faster as the coordinator node considers write success when any one node respond operation as a success, or a hinted handoff is written. A hinted handoff can be written even if all replica nodes are down. However, data written cannot be read until the replica nodes responsible for that data recover.

- SERIAL: This level should be used to write data using the LWT feature. Data is written on the nodes meeting the quorum based on the write condition mentioned in the LWT query.

- LOCAL_SERIAL: This is the same as SERIAL, but is only limited to the local datacenter.

Let's have a look at the following figure:

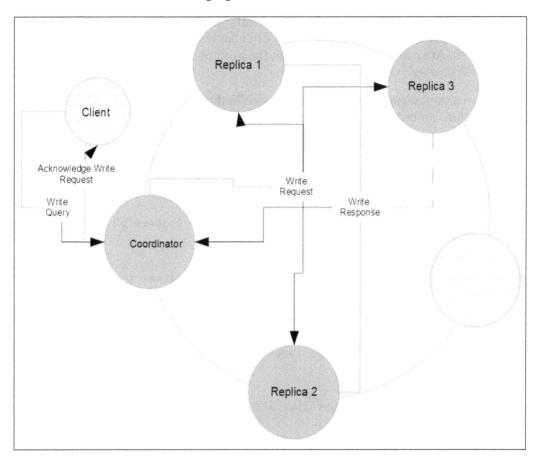

The preceding figure shows a write request on a five-node cluster with replication factor 3 and consistency level QUORUM. As can be seen, the write request is triggered towards all replica nodes by the coordinator. However, the coordinator node sends back an acknowledgement of the write operation to the client as soon as it gets write responses from Replica 1 and Replica 2. As the Replica 3 response reached late and was ignored, it is shown as a dashed line.

Tracing Cassandra queries

Cassandra allows us to trace a query session; this can be used to debug queries that perform badly. On the `cqlsh` prompt, you can enable tracing using the command `TRACING ON`. After that, each query run on the prompt will be traced, and the trace output will be displayed.

Cassandra automatically saves a traced session in the `system_traces` keyspace. A saved session can be referenced later on for up to 24 hours.

Take the example of tracing an `INSERT` statement. Let's first create a column family with replication factor 1, as shown in the following example. We're taking a low replication factor for the simplicity of the example. In our example, `10.78.171.11` is the coordinator node and `10.78.171.12` is the replica node:

```
cqlsh> CREATE KEYSPACE userdb WITH replication = {'class':
'SimpleStrategy' , 'replication_factor': 1};

cqlsh> USE userdb ;

cqlsh:userdb> CREATE TABLE users ( userid text, address text, PRIMARY
KEY(userid));

cqlsh:userdb> TRACING ON ;

Now Tracing is enabled

cqlsh:userdb> INSERT INTO users (userid, address ) VALUES ( 'nitinp',
'sec-18');


Tracing session: add23a10-eb59-11e4-a51b-811a5d39e8fc


 activity
| timestamp                      | source       | source_elapsed
---------------------------------------------------------------------
--------------------------+-------------------------------+---------------+---
-------------

Execute CQL3 query | 2015-04-25 20:15:12.920000 | 10.78.171.11 |
0

 Parsing INSERT INTO users (userid, address ) VALUES ( 'nitinp', 'sec-
18'); [SharedPool-Worker-1] | 2015-04-25 20:15:12.938000 | 10.78.171.11
|         52605

                                                      Preparing
statement [SharedPool-Worker-1] | 2015-04-25 20:15:12.943000 |
10.78.171.11 |         57693
```

```
                                        Determining replicas
for mutation [SharedPool-Worker-1] | 2015-04-25 20:15:12.960000 |
10.78.171.11 |          74540

                                        Sending message to
/10.78.171.12 [WRITE-/10.78.171.12] | 2015-04-25 20:15:12.993000 |
10.78.171.11 |          107516

                                        Message received from
/10.78.171.12 [Thread-20] | 2015-04-25 20:15:13.007000 | 10.78.171.11 |
121140

                                        Processing response from
/10.78.171.12 [SharedPool-Worker-3] | 2015-04-25 20:15:13.007000 |
10.78.171.11 |          121522

                                        Message received from
/10.78.171.11 [Thread-24] | 2015-04-25 20:15:29.142000 | 10.78.171.12
|          126

                                        Appending to
commitlog [SharedPool-Worker-1] | 2015-04-25 20:15:29.142000 |
10.78.171.12 |          462

                                        Adding to users
memtable [SharedPool-Worker-1] | 2015-04-25 20:15:29.142000 |
10.78.171.12 |          644

                                        Enqueuing response to
/10.78.171.11 [SharedPool-Worker-1] | 2015-04-25 20:15:29.143000 |
10.78.171.12 |          1320

                                        Sending message to
/10.78.171.11 [WRITE-/10.78.171.11] | 2015-04-25 20:15:29.143000 |
10.78.171.12 |          1526


Request complete | 2015-04-25 20:15:13.044637 | 10.78.171.11 |
124637
```

You can see in the preceding trace how the coordinator node first determines replicas responsible for storing the partition key nitinp, and then sends a write request to replica node 10.78.171.12. Upon receiving the request, replica node 10.78.171.12 appends it to the CommitLog and writes to the Memtable. It then sends a write request acknowledgement to coordinator 10.78.171.11 and upon receiving the message, coordinator 10.78.171.11, marks the request as complete.

Summary

In this chapter we've discussed what operations Cassandra performs internally when doing a Read or a Write operation. We discussed various key data structures which Cassandra maintains internally. We also discussed how these data structures and processes affects a read/write operation. We discussed the role of `CommitLog` to make a write operation durable also how it can be used to recover a data that is not flushed to disk yet and the node dies. Cassandra maintains different caches and employs various techniques like `BloomFilter` to make its read/write operation fast. It has various data consistency levels that can be tuned as per our needs. We've discussed how it first writes to memory to make write operation ultra-fast and then later on flushes that data to disk in the form of immutable `SSTables`. Since `SSTables` are immutables so over the time multiple SSTables are formed over a Cassandra node. Multiple SSTable for a column family could lead to multiple disks seeks for a read operation. Hence Cassandra employs technique called Compaction. There is different Compaction strategies available in Cassandra that could be chosen based on your data model.

5
Writing Your
Cassandra Client

There are many popular client drivers available for Java and other popular languages. You can find the list at `http://planetcassandra.org/client-drivers-tools/`. However, in this chapter we'll see how we can write our Cassandra client using the `Datastax` Java driver. This is one of the most popular drivers available, and we'll discuss some core features provided by it, such as the database connection pool support and various pool configuration options. We'll also discuss the mapping API provided by `Datastax`, which we can use to map Cassandra tables to our Java class objects. We'll also take a look at how we can enable tracing for queries from the Java driver.

Connecting to a Cassandra cluster

In order to make a connection with a Cassandra cluster, the `Cluster`, `Cluster.Builder`, and `Session` classes are used. The `Cluster` class can be used to connect to the cluster and fetch information about the cluster, like keyspaces, partitioner being used, all nodes in the cluster, the cluster name, and so on. While connecting, the class `Cluster.Builder` is used to specify cluster configuration options such as contact points, socket options, load balancing policy, retry policy, and so on.

In our example we're using Cassandra driver version 2.1.4 following are dependency details for our code examples:

```
private void connect() {
        Cluster cluster = Cluster.builder()
                        .addContactPoint("127.0.0.1")
                        .build();
// session variable is an instace of Session Class
        session = cluster.connect();
}
```

In the following example, we connect to a cluster with a contact point at the local machine using loopback address `127.0.0.1`:

```
private void connect() {
        Cluster cluster = Cluster.builder()
                        .addContactPoint("127.0.0.1")
                        .build();
// session variable is an instace of Session Class
        session = cluster.connect();
}
```

Here we're storing session instance as returned by `cluster.connect()` method in Class data member named session. We'll see its definition in full code snippet shown later in the chapter.

Contact points are needed by the Cassandra driver to discover the network topology. One contact point is good enough for this purpose, but it is recommended that you use more than one to ensure that, even if one contact point is down, driver initialization doesn't fail. If multiple nodes are given as contact points, the first node contacted will be considered the node local to the client, so it's recommended that, in a multiple datacenter environment, only those nodes in the same datacenter as the client should be given as contact points.

Successful connection to the cluster returns a session object. Session objects are thread-safe, and it is recommended that you use one session per application/ `keyspace`. A session holds a pool of connections to the Cassandra cluster. For every connected host, there is a connection pool. Each connection pool holds at least one connection based on the native protocol version used for connecting to Cassandra cluster. For example, native protocol version 2 can have more than one connection per connected host pool and can be configured. However, in native protocol version 3, only one connection is maintained per host pool. The following figure shows the relationship among the `Session`, `Pool`, and `Connection` objects:

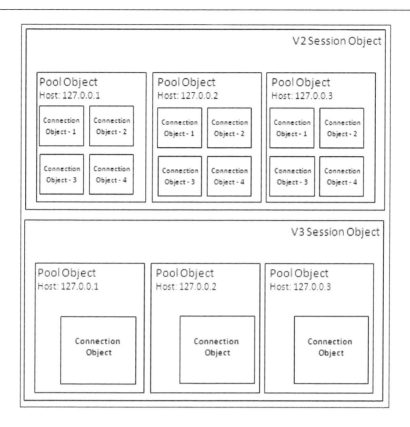

Each `connection` object can serve multiple simultaneous queries. In native protocol version 2, a maximum of 128 simultaneous queries are possible per connection object. In native protocol version 3, this can go up to 32,768 queries per connection object.

Now let's create a method `getClusterInfo()` to get our cluster information, such as the protocol version and connection objects, for each host:

```
public void getClusterInfo(Cluster cluster) {
   ProtocolOptions protocolOptions = cluster.getConfiguration().
getProtocolOptions();
   ProtocolVersion protocolVersion = protocolOptions.
getProtocolVersionEnum();
   Session.State state = session.getState();
   for ( Host host: state.getConnectedHosts()) {
     int connections = state.getOpenConnections(host);
     System.out.println("Host" + host + " Protocol Version: " +
protocolVersion +
        " Connections: " + connections );
   }
}
```

The native protocol version supported depends on the Cassandra version. The following table shows the native protocol version compatibility matrix:

	Cassandra 1.2.X	Cassandra 2.0.X	Cassandra 2.1.X
Datastax Driver 1.0.X	Version 1	Version 1	Version 1
Driver 2.0.X-2.1.1	Version 1	Version 1	Version 1
Driver 2.1.2 and above	Version 1	Version 2	Version 3

The connection pool configuration can be done using the `PoolingOptions` class object. The following code snippet sets maximum simultaneous requests per host for a V3 protocol connection, and maximum simultaneous requests for all connection objects of a host for V2 protocol for nodes that are marked as local nodes to 500. We've discussed how nodes are marked `local` or `remote` while discussing contact points. Note that both versions have different methods due to a difference in their nature; for example, V3 has only one connection object per host, while V2 can have many connection objects per host:

```
ProtocolOptions protocolOptions = cluster.getConfiguration().
getProtocolOptions();
PoolingOptions poolingOptions = new PoolingOptions();
ProtocolVersion protocolVersion = protocolOptions.
getProtocolVersionEnum();
if (protocolVersion == ProtocolVersion.V3) {
   poolingOptions.setMaxSimultaneousRequestsPerHostThreshold(HostDistan
ce.LOCAL, 500);
} else {
   poolingOptions.setMaxSimultaneousRequestsPerConnectionThreshold(Host
Distance.LOCAL, 500);
}
```

Driver Connection policies

Cassandra Java driver lets us define various policies for load balancing, retry mechanism in case a query fails and reconnection policies in case session with some node is disconnected. Let's discuss them in detail, we're discussing here various policies available in driver version 2.x.

Load balancing policies

The `Datastax` driver provides an interface that can be implemented to specify which nodes to contact for each new query. It requires the following two methods to be implemented:

1. `newQueryPlan()`

   ```
   Iterator<Host> newQueryPlan(String loggedKeyspace, Statement
   statement)
   ```

   This method returns a list of nodes that should be contacted for a query. The very first node on the list will be contacted first, and the next will be called in case of error.

2. `distance()`

   ```
   HostDistance distance(Host host)
   ```

   This method indicates whether or not the node returned by the `newQueryPlan()` method is `local` or `remote` from the client.

The `Datastax` driver provides the following preimplemented policies:

1. `RoundRobinPolicy`: This policy queries nodes in round-robin order. If a node connection fails during a query, it tries to connect to the next host. In this policy, the node queried could be in a remote data center in a multi-datacenter environment.

2. `DCAwareRoundRobinPolicy`: This is the same as `RoundRobinPolicy`, except that this policy guarantees that no host in remote data will be queried unless connections to all hosts in the local datacenter fail.

3. `LatencyAwarePolicy`: This policy is used as a wrapper over other policies; for example, it can be used with the `RoundRobinPolicy`. It adds latency awareness to its sub policies. To add latency awareness, it gives scores to each node based on the latencies of queries. If a node is found to be underperforming in comparison with ideal node performance by a predefined exclusion threshold, that node is removed from the list of nodes which should be contacted to query. An excluded node can be added back to the list after a period set by the method with retry period (long retry period; `TimeUnit` unit).

   ```
   public LatencyAwarePolicy.Builder withRetryPeriod(long
   retryPeriod, TimeUnit unit)
   ```

4. `TokenAwarePolicy`: This policy is also a wrapper policy. It adds token awareness to its sub policies. It returns a list of nodes to contact, with replica nodes of data queried at the head of a list if they are `LOCAL` to the contacted host.

5. `WhiteListPolicy`: This policy returns a list of nodes to be contacted to those hosts that are provided in its whitelist. However, the order of nodes in the returned list will be decided by its child policy.

The following code snippet creates a `LatencyAwarePolicy` with `RoundRobinPolicy` as its subpolicy:

```
LoadBalancingPolicy lbPolicy = LatencyAwarePolicy.builder(
    new RoundRobinPolicy()).build();
```

Retry policies

Retry policies define what default behavior to adopt when a request fails due to a `TimeoutException` or `UnavailableException`. Driver has the following predefined behavior that can be used:

1. `DefaultRetryPolicy`: This policy retries queries once when read or write timeout occurs. Query options used during retry will be the same as used while querying for the first time.

2. `DowngradingConsistencyRetryPolicy`: Similar to `DefaultRetryPolicy`, this policy retries queries on timeouts. However, one exception is that it could downgrade the consistency level while retrying if the original request has timed out because the number of replicas responding is lower than what was required by the consistency level of the original request.

3. `FallthroughRetryPolicy`: This policy doesn't retry; it will just `rethrow()` exceptions and business logic needed to catch and implement any decision that is required.

4. `LoggingRetryPolicy`: This is a wrapper policy. It takes actions as defined in its subpolicy. In addition to that, it logs the decision made by its subpolicy.

Reconnection policies

Reconnection policies define when to retry connecting to a node that was declared dead earlier. The following two policies are predefined:

1. `ConstantReconnectionPolicy`: The wait time between reconnection attempts is constant.

2. `ExponentialReconnectionPolicy`: The wait time increases exponentially, starting with a given base time and increasing towards a given maximum time.

Now, let's update the `connect()` method to incorporate our custom connection policies. The following code shows the updated `connect()` method with `PoolingOption` and `LoadBalancingPolicy` customizations. We've also added a `getSession()` method, which we'll be using to `getSession()` object, as shown here:

```
private static void connect() {
  PoolingOptions opts = new PoolingOptions();
  opts.setMaxSimultaneousRequestsPerHostThreshold(HostDistance.LOCAL,
500);
  LoadBalancingPolicy lbPolicy = LatencyAwarePolicy.builder(
      new RoundRobinPolicy()).build();
  Cluster cluster = Cluster.builder()
          .addContactPoint("127.0.0.1")
          .withPoolingOptions(opts)
          .withLoadBalancingPolicy(lbPolicy)
          .build();
  session = cluster.connect();

}

public static synchronized Session getSession() {
  if (session == null || session.isClosed()) {
    connect();
  }
  return session;
}
```

Reading and writing to the Cassandra cluster

We're able to connect to our Cassandra server. Now let's write some data to it and read it back. The `Session` class provides a method called `execute()`, which is used to send read/write queries to Cassandra and get the result set back.

We can use CQL statements in the `execute` statement as strings. In the following example, we create a function that will create `keyspace` and a table for us. We're using CQL statements for creating `keyspace` and tables as string arguments to the `execute` method. Fetch the `Session` object by using the `getSession()` method created earlier, as follows:

```
public static void createSchema() {
  // create keyspace
  getSession().execute(
    "CREATE KEYSPACE IF NOT EXISTS apachecassandra "
    + "WITH replication = {'class':'SimpleStrategy', 'replication_
```

```
factor':1 "
    + "};");
    // create table
    getSession().execute(
        "CREATE TABLE IF NOT EXISTS apachecassandra"
        + ".status_updates_by_user (" + "userid UUID,"
        + "updated_on timestamp," + "status text,"
        + "PRIMARY KEY (userid)" + ");");
}
```

This will prepare our database schema. Now, let's create methods to populate our table. The following method will insert a row in table `status_updates_by_user` for a given `userid` variable and user's status message. The time of creating the status will be the time when status is written:

```
public static void createStatus(String userId, String statusMsg) {
    String insertStatement = "INSERT INTO apachecassandra"
    + ".status_updates_by_user "
    + "(userid, updated_on, status) "
    + "VALUES (" + UUID.fromString(userId) + ","
    + "'" + System.currentTimeMillis() + "',"
    + "'" + statusMsg + "'"
        + ");";
    getSession().execute(insertStatement);


}
```

Here is the method for reading data populated by the `createStatus()` method. It first prepares a `SELECT` query in form of a `String` object. Then `session.execute()` is called with this string object as argument. Successful execution will return a `ResultSet` of rows as fetched by the `SELECT` query. We fetch this in our `FOR` loop using the `Row` object, and print each row's individual column values, as shown here:

```
public static void printStatus(String userId) {
    String selectStatement = "SELECT userid, updated_on, status FROM "
        + "apachecassandra.status_updates_by_user "
        + "WHERE userid = " + UUID.fromString(userId)
        + ";";
    ResultSet userStatus = getSession().execute(selectStatement);
    for(Row row: userStatus) {
        System.out.println("userId: " + row.getUUID("userid")
            + " update on " + row.getDate("updated_on")
            + " Status Message: " + row.getString("status"));
    }
}
```

Both the preceding methods create read and write queries and then provide them to the `execute()` method. The `Execute()` method runs the provided queries and blocks until some data is received from the database. `ResultSet` is never null, but can be empty; for example, for our `INSERT` query it is empty.

QueryBuilder

In the methods we just created, we're creating CQL statements as hard coded `String` objects. However, the driver also provides an interface called `QueryBuilder`, which can be used to generate read/write queries instead of hard coding them. Now let's rewrite the preceding methods using `QueryBuilder`:

```
public static void createStatus(String userId, String statusMsg) {
   Statement insertStatement = QueryBuilder
      .insertInto("apachecassandra", "status_updates_by_user")
      .value("userid", UUID.fromString(userId))
      .value("updated_on", System.currentTimeMillis())
      .value("status", statusMsg);
   getSession().execute(insertStatement);

}

public static void printStatus(String userId) {
   Statement selectStatement = QueryBuilder.select().column("userid")
      .column("updated_on").column("status")
      .from("apachecassandra", "status_updates_by_user")
      .where(QueryBuilder.eq("userid", UUID.fromString(userId)));
   ResultSet userStatus = getSession().execute(selectStatement);
   for (Row row : userStatus) {
     System.out.println("userId: " + row.getUUID("userid")
         + " update on " + row.getDate("updated_on")
         + " Status Message: " + row.getString("status"));
   }
}
```

As you can see, we aren't creating `SELECT` or `INSERT` queries using query builder. We're just providing input to `QueryBuilder` about what operation we want to perform so that `QueryBuilder` will then create CQL statements based on the inputs provided. Later on, we pass the statement generated by `QueryBuilder` to the `execute()` method as we were doing earlier.

Reading and writing asynchronously

As we've discussed, `Session.execute()` is a blocking function that doesn't unblock until some data or error is returned by Cassandra cluster. This could be a scenario in which we know the query we're executing could take some time. By the time the query is complete, we want to execute some other business logic, and then, later on, fetch results returned by query. For such scenarios, the driver provides the `executeAsync()` method, which returns the `ResultSetFuture` object instead of `ResultSet`.

 Any failures while executing a query (for example, an invalid query exception) are not thrown when we call the `executeAsync()` method. Those should be handled when we access the `ResultSetFuture` object.

In the following code, we see our `selectStatus()` method running the SELECT query for status messages asynchronously. In this method, we first prepare by telling `QueryBuilder` to prepare our SELECT query to fetch a complete row for a given `userid` variable. Then, we execute this query asynchronously. At this point, our code doesn't wait until the result of the query is fetched, but returns immediately with the `ResultSetFuture` object. Then, we perform some other dummy business logic, which in our case is sleeping for five seconds. When that method is returned, we check the results of the query we executed earlier. Upon successful execution, this will print all column values for the user with the given `userid` variable:

```
public static void printStatusAsync(String userId) {
  Statement selectStatement = QueryBuilder.select().column("userid")
.column("updated_on").column("status")
      .from("apachecassandra", "status_updates_by_user")
      .where(QueryBuilder.eq("userid", UUID.fromString(userId)));
  // don't block here
  ResultSetFuture userStatusFuture = getSession().executeAsync(
      selectStatement);
  // do some other business logic here
  doSomeOtherBusinessStuff();
  // fetch result set
  ResultSet userStatus;
  try {
    userStatus = userStatusFuture.get();
    System.out.println("Async Result");
    for (Row row : userStatus) {
      System.out.println("userId: " + row.getUUID("userid")
          + " update on " + row.getDate("updated_on")
          + " Status Message: " + row.getString("status"));
```

```
      }
    } catch (InterruptedException e) {
      e.printStackTrace();
    } catch (ExecutionException e) {
      e.printStackTrace();
    }
  }

  public static void doSomeOtherBusinessStuff() {
    try {
      Thread.sleep(5000);
    } catch (InterruptedException e) {
      e.printStackTrace();
    }
  }
}
```

The following is the complete sample program with all the methods we've discussed:

```
package apachecassandra.client;

import java.util.UUID;
import java.util.concurrent.ExecutionException;

import com.datastax.driver.core.Cluster;
import com.datastax.driver.core.Host;
import com.datastax.driver.core.HostDistance;
import com.datastax.driver.core.PoolingOptions;
import com.datastax.driver.core.ProtocolOptions;
import com.datastax.driver.core.ProtocolVersion;
import com.datastax.driver.core.ResultSet;
import com.datastax.driver.core.ResultSetFuture;
import com.datastax.driver.core.Row;
import com.datastax.driver.core.Session;
import com.datastax.driver.core.Statement;
import com.datastax.driver.core.policies.LatencyAwarePolicy;
import com.datastax.driver.core.policies.LoadBalancingPolicy;
import com.datastax.driver.core.policies.RoundRobinPolicy;
import com.datastax.driver.core.querybuilder.QueryBuilder;

public class CassandraClient {
  private static Session session = null;

  private void connect() {
    PoolingOptions opts = new PoolingOptions();
```

```
        opts.setMaxSimultaneousRequestsPerHostThreshold(HostDistance.LOCAL,
    500);
        LoadBalancingPolicy lbPolicy = LatencyAwarePolicy.builder(
            new RoundRobinPolicy()).build();
        Cluster cluster = Cluster.builder().addContactPoint("127.0.0.1")
            .withPoolingOptions(opts).withLoadBalancingPolicy(lbPolicy)
            .build();
        session = cluster.connect();
        getClusterInfo(cluster);


    }

    public void getClusterInfo(Cluster cluster) {
        ProtocolOptions protocolOptions = cluster.getConfiguration()
            .getProtocolOptions();
        ProtocolVersion protocolVersion = protocolOptions
            .getProtocolVersionEnum();
        Session.State state = session.getState();
        for (Host host : state.getConnectedHosts()) {
            int connections = state.getOpenConnections(host);
            System.out.println("Host"
                + host
                + " Protocol Version: "
                + protocolVersion
                + " Connections: "
                + connections
                + " Reconnection Policy"
                + cluster.getConfiguration().getPolicies()
                    .getReconnectionPolicy().toString()
                + " Retry Policy"
                + cluster.getConfiguration().getPolicies().getRetryPolicy()
                    .toString()
                + " LoadBalancing Policy"
                + cluster.getConfiguration().getPolicies()
                    .getLoadBalancingPolicy().toString());

        }
    }

    public void createStatus(String userId, String statusMsg) {
        Statement insertStatement = QueryBuilder
            .insertInto("apachecassandra", "status_updates_by_user")
            .value("userid", UUID.fromString(userId))
            .value("updated_on", System.currentTimeMillis())
```

```
        .value("status", statusMsg);
    getSession().execute(insertStatement);


}


public void printStatus(String userId) {
    Statement selectStatement = QueryBuilder.select().column("userid")
        .column("updated_on").column("status")
        .from("apachecassandra", "status_updates_by_user")
        .where(QueryBuilder.eq("userid", UUID.fromString(userId)));
    ResultSet userStatus = getSession().execute(selectStatement);
    for (Row row : userStatus) {
      System.out.println("userId: " + row.getUUID("userid")
          + " update on " + row.getDate("updated_on")
          + " Status Message: " + row.getString("status"));
    }
}


public void printStatusAsync(String userId) {
    Statement selectStatement = QueryBuilder.select().column("userid")
        .column("updated_on").column("status")
        .from("apachecassandra", "status_updates_by_user")
        .where(QueryBuilder.eq("userid", UUID.fromString(userId)));
    // don't block here
    ResultSetFuture userStatusFuture = getSession().executeAsync(
        selectStatement);
    // do some other business logic here
    doSomeOtherBusinessStuff();
    // fetch result set
    ResultSet userStatus;
    try {
      userStatus = userStatusFuture.get();
      System.out.println("Async Result");
      for (Row row : userStatus) {
        System.out.println("userId: " + row.getUUID("userid")
            + " update on " + row.getDate("updated_on")
            + " Status Message: " + row.getString("status"));
      }
    } catch (InterruptedException e) {
      e.printStackTrace();
    } catch (ExecutionException e) {
      e.printStackTrace();
    }
}
```

```java
    public void doSomeOtherBusinessStuff() {
      try {
        Thread.sleep(5000);
      } catch (InterruptedException e) {
        e.printStackTrace();
      }
    }

    public Session getSession() {
      if (session == null || session.isClosed()) {
        connect();
      }
      return session;
    }

    public void createSchema() {

      // create keyspace
      getSession().execute(
          "CREATE KEYSPACE IF NOT EXISTS apachecassandra WITH
replication = "
            + "{'class':'SimpleStrategy', 'replication_factor':1 "
            + "};");
      // create table
      getSession().execute(
          "CREATE TABLE IF NOT EXISTS apachecassandra"
            + ".status_updates_by_user (" + "userid UUID,"
            + "updated_on timestamp," + "status text,"
            + "PRIMARY KEY (userid) );");

    }

    public static void main(String[] args) {
      CassandraClient client = new CassandraClient();
      client.createSchema();

      client.createStatus("de305d54-75b4-431b-adb2-eb6b9e546014",
          "my message");
      client.printStatus("de305d54-75b4-431b-adb2-eb6b9e546014");
      client.printStatusAsync("de305d54-75b4-431b-adb2-eb6b9e546014");
    }
  }
```

Prepared statements

Prepared statements provide a slight performance gain over normal statement execution for queries that run frequently, as these statements are parsed only once by Cassandra and can be executed multiple times.

For example, we can prepare an `INSERT` statement for the user status during application startup, and that prepared statement can later be bound to actual values and executed multiple times.

We can create a prepared statement using the `Session` object's `prepare()` method:

```
PreparedStatement setStatusStatement = getSession()
        .prepare(
            "INSERT INTO "
            + "apachecassandra.status_updates_by_user "
            + "(userid, updated_on, status) "
            + "VALUES (?, ?, ?);");
```

Later on, this session is bound to actual values and then executed using the `Session` object's `execute()` method:

```
getSession().execute(setStatusStatement.bind(
        UUID.fromString("de305d54-75b4-431b-adb2-eb6b9e546014"),
        System.currentTimeMillis(),
        "Hello World"
        ) );
```

Example REST service using prepared statement

To demonstrate this, let's take the example of a REST service that provides APIs to set a user's status and get user's latest status update. In our example, we've created a Data Access Object class called `UserStatusDAO`, which provides methods to create and read a user status. This class is listed here:

StatusDAO.java:

```
package cassandra.cassandraclient.db;

import java.util.UUID;

import cassandra.cassandraclient.model.Status;

public interface StatusDAO {

  // Get a user's latest status
```

```
        Status get(UUID userID);
        // Set a user status
        void set(Status userStatus);

}
```

The following class implements interface `StatusDAO`. This class is named `StatusDAOImpl`, as shown here:

StatusDAOImpl.java

```java
package cassandra.cassandraclient.db;

import java.util.UUID;

import cassandra.cassandraclient.model.Status;

import com.datastax.driver.core.PreparedStatement;
import com.datastax.driver.core.ResultSet;
import com.datastax.driver.core.Row;

public class StatusDAOImpl implements StatusDAO {

  private static PreparedStatement setStatusStatement = null;
  private static PreparedStatement getStatusStatement = null;

  public Status get(UUID userID) {
    PreparedStatement getStmt = getGetStatusStatement();
    Status statusMsg = null;
    if (getStmt != null) {
      ResultSet rsStatusDetails = ConnectionHelper.getSession().
execute(
          getStmt.bind(userID));
      statusMsg = new Status();
      for (Row row : rsStatusDetails) {
        statusMsg.setUserId(row.getUUID("userid"));
        statusMsg.setUpdatedOn(row.getDate("updated_on"));
        statusMsg.setStausMsg(row.getString("status"));
      }
    }

    return statusMsg;
  }

  public void set(Status userStatus) {
    PreparedStatement setStmt = getSetStatusStatement();
```

```
      if (setStmt != null) {
        ConnectionHelper.getSession()
            .execute(
                setStmt.bind(userStatus.getUserId(),
                    userStatus.getUpdatedOn(),
                    userStatus.getStausMsg()));
    }
  }

  public static void prepareSetStatusStatement() {
    setStatusStatement = ConnectionHelper.getSession()
        .prepare(
            "INSERT INTO "
                + "apachecassandra.status_updates_by_user "
                + "(userid, updated_on, status) "
                + "VALUES (?, ?, ?);");
  }

  public static PreparedStatement getSetStatusStatement() {
    return setStatusStatement;
  }

  public static void prepareGetStatusStatement() {
    getStatusStatement = ConnectionHelper.getSession().prepare(
        "SELECT userid, updated_on, status FROM "
            + "apachecassandra.status_updates_by_user "
            + "WHERE userid = ? "
            + " ORDER BY updated_ON DESC LIMIT 1;");
  }

  public static PreparedStatement getGetStatusStatement() {
    return getStatusStatement;
  }

}
```

In our implementation class, StatusDAOImpl, we've defined two helper methods,
prepareSetStatusStatement() and prepareGetStatusStatement(). These
methods are used to create and set prepared statements for the INSERT and SELECT
statements to insert and get a user's status update, respectively.

These methods can be called during application startup time. Later on, whenever a `get()` or `set()` request comes, the `get()` and `set()` methods will bind them to the provided values and execute them. Since ours is a REST app, one of the ways of preparing these statements could be during context initialization, as shown here:

```
package cassandra.cassandraclient.listeners;

import javax.servlet.ServletContextEvent;
import javax.servlet.ServletContextListener;

import cassandra.cassandraclient.db.ConnectionHelper;
import cassandra.cassandraclient.db.StatusDAOImpl;

public class CassandraClientServletListener implements
ServletContextListener {

  public void contextDestroyed(ServletContextEvent arg0) {
    // TODO Auto-generated method stub

  }

  public void contextInitialized(ServletContextEvent
servletContextEvent) {
    // Create Database Schema
    ConnectionHelper.createSchema();

    // Preapare INSERT and SELECT statements
    StatusDAOImpl.prepareSetStatusStatement();
    StatusDAOImpl.prepareGetStatusStatement();
  }

}
```

For our REST service, we've created a class, `ConnectionHelper`, to provide Cassandra connection functions. This class is listed here:

ConnectionHelper.java
```
package cassandra.cassandraclient.db;

import com.datastax.driver.core.Cluster;
import com.datastax.driver.core.Session;

public final class ConnectionHelper {
  private static Session session = null;
```

```
    private static void connect() {
      Cluster cluster = Cluster.builder().addContactPoint("127.0.0.1")
          .build();
      session = cluster.connect();

    }

    public static synchronized Session getSession() {
      if (session == null || session.isClosed()) {
        connect();
      }
      return session;
    }

    public static void createSchema() {

      // create keyspace
      getSession().execute(
          "CREATE KEYSPACE IF NOT EXISTS apachecassandra WITH
  replication = "
              + "{'class':'SimpleStrategy', 'replication_factor':1 "
              + "};");
      // create table
      getSession().execute(
          "CREATE TABLE IF NOT EXISTS apachecassandra"
              + ".status_updates_by_user (" + "userid UUID,"
              + "updated_on timestamp," + "status text,"
              + "PRIMARY KEY (userid) );");
    }

}
```

Here is our Status class representing a Status object for a user:

Status.java
```
package cassandra.cassandraclient.model;

import java.util.Date;
import java.util.UUID;

import com.datastax.driver.mapping.annotations.Column;
import com.datastax.driver.mapping.annotations.PartitionKey;
import com.datastax.driver.mapping.annotations.Table;

public class Status {
```

```java
      private UUID userId;

      private Date updatedOn;

      private String stausMsg;

      public Status() {

      }

      public UUID getUserId() {
        return userId;
      }

      public void setUserId(UUID userId) {
        this.userId = userId;
      }

      public Date getUpdatedOn() {
        return updatedOn;
      }

      public void setUpdatedOn(Date updatedOn) {
        this.updatedOn = updatedOn;
      }

      public String getStausMsg() {
        return stausMsg;
      }

      public void setStausMsg(String stausMsg) {
        this.stausMsg = stausMsg;
      }
    }
```

Below is our REST status resource class which is reading and writing status updates of a user:

```java
//StatusResource.java
package cassandra.cassandraclient.resources;

import java.util.List;
import java.util.UUID;

import javax.ws.rs.Consumes;
```

```
import javax.ws.rs.GET;
import javax.ws.rs.POST;
import javax.ws.rs.Path;
import javax.ws.rs.PathParam;
import javax.ws.rs.Produces;
import javax.ws.rs.core.MediaType;

import cassandra.cassandraclient.db.StatusDAO;
import cassandra.cassandraclient.db.StatusDAOImpl;
import cassandra.cassandraclient.model.Status;

@Path("/v1/status")
public class StatusResource {
        @GET
        @Path("{userId}")
        @Produces(MediaType.APPLICATION_JSON)
        public Status getUserStat(@PathParam("userId") UUID userID) {
                StatusDAO dao = new StatusDAOImpl();
                Status userStatus = dao.get(userID);
                return userStatus;
        }
        @POST
        @Path("{userId}")
        @Produces(MediaType.APPLICATION_JSON)
        @Consumes(MediaType.APPLICATION_JSON)
         public Status setUserStat(@PathParam("userId") UUID userId,
                      Status userStatus) {
    userStatus.setUserId(userId);
    StatusDAO dao = new StatusDAOImpl();
    dao.set(userStatus);
    return userStatus;
        }

}
```

Batch statements

In *Chapter 3, Creating Database and Schema*, we discussed how, in some scenarios, batch statements can save query execution time by sending multiple related queries in a single batch. We can run batch statements using a Java driver as well. Here is a snippet showing this:

```
public void batchOperation() {
    getSession().execute(
        "BEGIN BATCH   "
```

```
       + "  INSERT INTO cars (brand, model, variant , body_type,
colors, mileage) "
       + "  VALUES ( 'Audi', 'Q1', '3.0 TDI QUATTRO', 'Sedan',
{'Apple Green', 'Titanium Black'}, 14.2); "
       + "  UPDATE cars SET body_type = 'Sedan' WHERE brand='Audi' "
       + "  AND model ='Q7' AND variant = '3.0 TDI QUATTRO PREMIUM
PLUS'; "
       + "APPLY BATCH"
       );
   }
```

Mapping API

The Datastax Java driver provides a mapping API that helps to map our query results to Java classes. This API is provided as a separate artifact. We're using mapping API version 2.1.4 in our examples, below are dependency details:

```
// Maven Dependancy
<dependency>
    <groupId>com.datastax.cassandra</groupId>
    <artifactId>cassandra-driver-mapping</artifactId>
    <version>2.1.4</version>
</dependency>
// Gradle Dependancy
compile 'com.datastax.cassandra:Cassandra-driver-mapping:2.1.4'
```

The mapping API provides annotations to map a Java class to a Cassandra table. For example, our Status class can be mapped to Cassandra table status_updates_ by_user, as in the following example of Status.java, updated as per the mapping API:

```
package cassandra.cassandraclient.model;

import java.util.Date;
import java.util.UUID;

import com.datastax.driver.mapping.annotations.Column;
import com.datastax.driver.mapping.annotations.PartitionKey;
import com.datastax.driver.mapping.annotations.Table;

/**
 * Status.java is mapped to below table schema
 * CREATE TABLE status_updates_by_user (
 * userid uuid,
 * status text,
```

```
 * updated_on timestamp,
 * PRIMARY KEY ((userid))
 * )
*/

@Table(keyspace = "apachecassandra", name = "status_updates_by_user")
public class Status {
  @PartitionKey
  private UUID userId;

  @Column(name = "updated_on")
  private Date updatedOn;

  @Column(name = "status")
  private String stausMsg;

  public Status() {

  }

  public UUID getUserId() {
    return userId;
  }

  public void setUserId(UUID userId) {
    this.userId = userId;
  }

  public Date getUpdatedOn() {
    return updatedOn;
  }

  public void setUpdatedOn(Date updatedOn) {
    this.updatedOn = updatedOn;
  }

  public String getStausMsg() {
    return stausMsg;
  }

  public void setStausMsg(String stausMsg) {
    this.stausMsg = stausMsg;
  }
}
```

As you can see, the @Table annotation is used to map the Cassandra table to our Status class. @PartitionKey says that the userId field is the partition key of the table. Since there is no clustering key, this will be the primary key as well. @ClusteringColumn would have been used if we had any clustering column. Note that we've used the @Column annotation for data members updatedOn and statusMsg, because our table name columns are different - updated_on, and status, respectively. If the Java class data members name is the same as the Cassandra column name, there is no need to use @Column.

In order to perform basic CRUD operations - for example, get(), save(), and so on - we first need to create an instance of the Mapper class. A Mapper instance is created using MappingManager, as follows:

```
Mapper<T> mapper = new MappingManager(ConnectionHelper.getSession()).
mapper(T.class);
```

Here, T is the class which we want to map with. In our case, this is the Status class, so we'll create it as follows:

```
Mapper<Status> mapper = new MappingManager(ConnectionHelper.
getSession()).mapper(Status.class);
```

This Mapper instance will now be used to perform CRUD operations on the Status class. For example, we can fetch a row mapped to the Status object by using its primary key userId:

```
Status statusMsg = mapper.get(userID);
```

The following code listing implements StatusDAO using Mapper:

```
package cassandra.cassandraclient.db;

import java.util.UUID;

import cassandra.cassandraclient.model.Status;

import com.datastax.driver.core.PreparedStatement;
import com.datastax.driver.mapping.Mapper;
import com.datastax.driver.mapping.MappingManager;

public class StatusDAOImpl implements StatusDAO {

  public Status get(UUID userID) {
    Status statusMsg = null;
    Mapper<Status> mapper = new MappingManager(ConnectionHelper.
getSession()).mapper(Status.class);
    statusMsg = mapper.get(userID);
```

```
      return statusMsg;
  }

  public void set(Status userStatus) {
     Mapper<Status> mapper = new MappingManager(ConnectionHelper.
getSession()).mapper(Status.class);
     mapper.save(userStatus);
  }

}
```

If we want to perform complex queries other than basic CRUD operations, the driver provides the annotation @Accessor, which is used to define an interface where we can map our complex queries to interface methods. For example, in our StatusDAO class, if we wanted to perform get all status for all users, this would be done by creating an interface annotated with @Accessor. Here is our StatusAccessor interface mapped to SELECT all queries:

```
package cassandra.cassandraclient.db;

import cassandra.cassandraclient.model.Status;

import com.datastax.driver.mapping.Result;
import com.datastax.driver.mapping.annotations.Accessor;
import com.datastax.driver.mapping.annotations.Query;

@Accessor
public interface StatusAccessor {
  @Query("SELECT * FROM apachecassandra.status_updates_by_user")
  Result<Status> getAll();
}
```

Since our accessor is ready now, let's add a getAll() method in our StatusDAO interface, and then implement it in our StatusDAOImpl class in a getAll method, as follows:

```
public List<Status> getAll() {
   MappingManager manager = new MappingManager(
      ConnectionHelper.getSession());
   StatusAccessor statusAccessor = manager
      .createAccessor(StatusAccessor.class);
   List<Status> statusMsgs = statusAccessor.getAll().all();
   return statusMsgs;
}
```

Our `accessor` interface is of the returning type `Result<Status>`, which is an iterable class mapped to the `Status` class. Since we're returning list of status objects in our REST API implementation as a response of `GET all` operation, we're using the `all()` method of the `Result` class.

Here is a full implementation of `StatusDAO`, `StatuDAOImpl`, and `Rest Resource`, using these methods:

StatusDAO.java

```java
package cassandra.cassandraclient.db;

import java.util.List;
import java.util.UUID;

import cassandra.cassandraclient.model.Status;

import com.datastax.driver.mapping.annotations.Accessor;

@Accessor
public interface StatusDAO {

    Status get(UUID userID);

    void set(Status userStatus);

    List<Status> getAll();

}
```

StatusDAOImpl.java

```java
package cassandra.cassandraclient.db;

import java.util.List;
import java.util.UUID;

import cassandra.cassandraclient.model.Status;

import com.datastax.driver.core.PreparedStatement;
import com.datastax.driver.mapping.Mapper;
import com.datastax.driver.mapping.MappingManager;

public class StatusDAOImpl implements StatusDAO {

    public Status get(UUID userID) {
        Status statusMsg = null;
```

```java
    Mapper<Status> mapper = new MappingManager(
        ConnectionHelper.getSession()).mapper(Status.class);
    statusMsg = mapper.get(userID);
    return statusMsg;
  }

  public void set(Status userStatus) {
    Mapper<Status> mapper = new MappingManager(
        ConnectionHelper.getSession()).mapper(Status.class);
    mapper.save(userStatus);
  }

  public List<Status> getAll() {
    MappingManager manager = new MappingManager(
        ConnectionHelper.getSession());
    StatusAccessor statusAccessor = manager
        .createAccessor(StatusAccessor.class);
    List<Status> statusMsgs = statusAccessor.getAll().all();
    return statusMsgs;
  }

}
```

StatusResource.java

```java
package cassandra.cassandraclient.resources;

import java.util.List;
import java.util.UUID;

import javax.ws.rs.Consumes;
import javax.ws.rs.GET;
import javax.ws.rs.POST;
import javax.ws.rs.Path;
import javax.ws.rs.PathParam;
import javax.ws.rs.Produces;
import javax.ws.rs.core.MediaType;

import cassandra.cassandraclient.db.StatusDAO;
import cassandra.cassandraclient.db.StatusDAOImpl;
import cassandra.cassandraclient.model.Status;

@Path("/v1/status")
public class StatusResource {

  @GET
```

```
@Path("{userId}")
@Produces(MediaType.APPLICATION_JSON)
public Status getUserStat(@PathParam("userId") UUID userID) {
  StatusDAO dao = new StatusDAOImpl();
  Status userStatus = dao.get(userID);
  return userStatus;
}


@GET
@Produces(MediaType.APPLICATION_JSON)
public List<Status> getAllStat() {
  StatusDAO dao = new StatusDAOImpl();
  List<Status> userStatus = dao.getAll();
  return userStatus;
}


@POST
@Path("{userId}")
@Produces(MediaType.APPLICATION_JSON)
@Consumes(MediaType.APPLICATION_JSON)
public Status setUserStat(@PathParam("userId") UUID userId,
    Status userStatus) {
  userStatus.setUserId(userId);
  StatusDAO dao = new StatusDAOImpl();
  dao.set(userStatus);
  return userStatus;
}

}
```

Tracing Cassandra queries using Java driver

We discussed tracing in the previous chapter, so you know how we can trace a query using the cqlsh client. Similarly, we can enable tracing on a per-query basis using driver as well. The following code shows a new version of our createStatus() method, with tracing enabled:

```
public void traceCreateStatus(String userId, String statusMsg) {
    Statement insertStatement = QueryBuilder
        .insertInto("apachecassandra", "status_updates_by_user")
        .value("userid", UUID.fromString(userId))
        .value("updated_on", System.currentTimeMillis())
```

```
        .value("status", statusMsg)
        .enableTracing();
    ResultSet rs = getSession().execute(insertStatement);
    ExecutionInfo executionInfo = rs.getExecutionInfo();
    QueryTrace queryTrace = executionInfo.getQueryTrace();
      System.out.println("Trace id: " + queryTrace.getTraceId());
      for (QueryTrace.Event event : queryTrace.getEvents()) {
        System.out.printf("%120s | %12s | %10s | %12s\n", event.
getDescription(),
                event.getTimestamp(),
                event.getSource(), event.getSourceElapsedMicros());
      }
  }
}
```

Here is the output after running the preceding method:

```
userId: de305d54-75b4-431b-adb2-eb6b9e14a014 update on Mon May 25
11:03:32 IST 2015 Status Message: my message
Trace id: 97fdb3b0-029f-11e5-b401-55ddb6596e18
        Parsing INSERT INTO apachecassandra.status_updates_by_
user(userid,updated_on,status) VALUES (?,1432532017770,?); |
1432532017771 | /127.0.0.1 |              60

Preparing statement | 1432532017771 | /127.0.0.1 |             135

Determining replicas for mutation | 1432532017771 | /127.0.0.1 |
225

Acquiring switchLock read lock | 1432532017771 | /127.0.0.1 |
286

Appending to commitlog | 1432532017771 | /127.0.0.1 |            295

Adding to status_updates_by_user memtable | 1432532017771 | /127.0.0.1
|            314
```

Summary

The Cassandra Java Driver Session object is a pool of connection objects. Typically, for most of the applications, one session object is sufficient per keyspace. We can customize pool configuration using the PoolingOptions object. While creating a Cluster object, we can customize load balancing, Reconnection policies, and Retry policies according to our needs. Read and write operations can be done both in synchronous and asynchronous manners. Prepared statements can provide a slight performance gain for queries which are executed frequently, as they are parsed only time by database. The mapping API can be used to map Java POJO classes to Cassandra tables. It enables APIs to perform basic CRUD operations on those POJO classes. For complex query operations, we need to create an interface annotated with the @Accessor annotation. We can enable tracing in Java Driver on a per-query basis.

6
Monitoring and Tuning a Cassandra Cluster

In this chapter, we'll discuss the various tools that can be used to monitor a Cassandra cluster. We'll discuss how to access Cassandra logs to fetch information that could be the cause of an issue we're debugging. We'll discuss various **nodetool** commands that are used to monitor the Cassandra server. We'll see how can we can attach **JConsole** to a Cassandra node and monitor the node remotely. In order to get improved performance from a Cassandra node, we might need to tune some of its aspects; for example, we might need to tune Java Heap's configurations or Cassandra cache settings. In the latter part of this chapter, we'll discuss these tuning topics.

Monitoring a Cassandra cluster

Monitoring is an important aspect of running our Cassandra server healthy and debugging and fine tuning it. Cassandra provides its activity information in the form of logs. It also captures various metrics that can be monitored using the JMX interface or **nodetool utility** provided by Cassandra. Let's discuss these in detail in the following sections.

Use logging for debugging

Cassandra logs its activities in a system log file called `system.log`. This file can be found at `<Cassandra-installation-director>/log` for tar-based installations and in the `/var/log/Cassandra` directory for package-based installations. Cassandra used the `Apache Log4j` library prior to version 2.1, and it has used the `Logback` library to dump logs since version 2.1. It uses various logging levels to log information appropriately. The default log level enabled is `INFO`, hence we can see various informational messages logged in this file. If a failure happens, then it'll also be logged in this file. For example, the following log snippet shows an error scenario where Cassandra was not able to load a saved cache during startup time:

```
INFO [main] 2015-01-06 18:29:47,098 AutoSavingCache.java:146 - reading saved cache dsc-cassandra-2.1.2/bin/../data/saved_caches/
apachecassandraexample-new_car_by_budget_key_cache-0acf01b089d711e4814bf1aeb6ca5530-RowCache-b.db
ERROR [main] 2015-01-06 18:29:47,133 CassandraDaemon.java:465 - Exception encountered during startup
java.lang.AssertionError: null
        at org.apache.cassandra.cache.SerializingCacheProvider$RowCacheSerializer.serialize(SerializingCacheProvider.java:41) ~[apache-cassandra-2.1.2.jar:2.1.2]
        at org.apache.cassandra.cache.SerializingCacheProvider$RowCacheSerializer.serialize(SerializingCacheProvider.java:37) ~[apache-cassandra-2.1.2.jar:2.1.2]
        at org.apache.cassandra.cache.SerializingCache.serialize(SerializingCache.java:118) ~[apache-cassandra-2.1.2.jar:2.1.2]
        at org.apache.cassandra.cache.SerializingCache.put(SerializingCache.java:177) ~[apache-cassandra-2.1.2.jar:2.1.2]
        at org.apache.cassandra.cache.InstrumentingCache.put(InstrumentingCache.java:44) ~[apache-cassandra-2.1.2.jar:2.1.2]
        at org.apache.cassandra.cache.AutoSavingCache.loadSaved(AutoSavingCache.java:163) ~[apache-cassandra-2.1.2.jar:2.1.2]
        at org.apache.cassandra.db.ColumnFamilyStore.initRowCache(ColumnFamilyStore.java:611) ~[apache-cassandra-2.1.2.jar:2.1.2]
        at org.apache.cassandra.db.Keyspace.open(Keyspace.java:127) ~[apache-cassandra-2.1.2.jar:2.1.2]
        at org.apache.cassandra.db.Keyspace.open(Keyspace.java:99) ~[apache-cassandra-2.1.2.jar:2.1.2]
        at org.apache.cassandra.service.CassandraDaemon.setup(CassandraDaemon.java:254) [apache-cassandra-2.1.2.jar:2.1.2]
        at org.apache.cassandra.service.CassandraDaemon.activate(CassandraDaemon.java:448) [apache-cassandra-2.1.2.jar:2.1.2]
        at org.apache.cassandra.service.CassandraDaemon.main(CassandraDaemon.java:537) [apache-cassandra-2.1.2.jar:2.1.2]
```

More detailed information can be seen if we set the log level to `DEBUG`, but since it'll do heavy I/O while logging this extra information, it's disabled by default and not recommended on production machines. For Cassandra versions prior to 2.1, logging configuration can be done in the `log4j-server.properties` file found in the `conf` directory of Cassandra installation; and from version 2.1 onwards, it is configured in the `logback.xml` file.

Monitoring using command-line utilities

The Cassandra command-line utility `nodetool` provides various commands to monitor a Cassandra node. These are discussed in following sections.

nodetool cfstats

The `cfstats` command is used to get the statistics of a Cassandra column family. We can monitor metrics such as read/write count and their respective latencies, memtable usage, and so on. The syntax for running the `nodetool cfstats` command is:

```
nodetool <connection-options> cfstats <keyspace-name>.<column-family-
name>
```

For example, to get the statistics of the column family `new_car_by_budget` in the keyspace `apachecassandraexample`, it can be run as shown in the following screenshot. Here, we've used the `-h 127.0.0.1` connection option to let the command know which node to query. In the following example, we're querying local nodes so we could've ignored that option:

```
$ nodetool -h 127.0.0.1 cfstats apachecassandraexample.new_car_by_budget
Keyspace: apachecassandraexample
        Read Count: 0
        Read Latency: NaN ms.
        Write Count: 0
        Write Latency: NaN ms.
        Pending Flushes: 0
                Table: new_car_by_budget
                SSTable count: 1
                Space used (live): 5429
                Space used (total): 5429
                Space used by snapshots (total): 0
                SSTable Compression Ratio: 0.312972972972973
                Memtable cell count: 0
                Memtable data size: 0
                Memtable switch count: 0
                Local read count: 0
                Local read latency: NaN ms
                Local write count: 0
                Local write latency: NaN ms
                Pending flushes: 0
                Bloom filter false positives: 0
                Bloom filter false ratio: 0.00000
                Bloom filter space used: 16
                Compacted partition minimum bytes: 1598
                Compacted partition maximum bytes: 1916
                Compacted partition mean bytes: 1916
                Average live cells per slice (last five minutes): 0.0
                Maximum live cells per slice (last five minutes): 0.0
                Average tombstones per slice (last five minutes): 0.0
                Maximum tombstones per slice (last five minutes): 0.0
```

As we can see in the output, the column family has one SSTable and there are no read and write operations performed yet. After running two read operations and one write operation on the column family, if we again run the command, the output will be similar as shown in the following screenshot. Here we can see that the read count is changed to 2 and the write count to changed to 1. Latency for the read count is 65 ms and the write latency is 0.38ms. We can see that Memtable cell count is also increased to 8 cells, which is the result of running our write operation:

```
$ nodetool -h 127.0.0.1 cfstats apachecassandraexample.new_car_by_budget
Keyspace: apachecassandraexample
        Read Count: 2
        Read Latency: 65.7565 ms.
        Write Count: 1
        Write Latency: 0.379 ms.
        Pending Flushes: 0
                Table: new_car_by_budget
                SSTable count: 1
                Space used (live): 5429
                Space used (total): 5429
                Space used by snapshots (total): 0
                SSTable Compression Ratio: 0.312972972972973
                Memtable cell count: 8
                Memtable data size: 237
                Memtable switch count: 0
                Local read count: 2
                Local read latency: 65.757 ms
                Local write count: 1
                Local write latency: 0.380 ms
                Pending flushes: 0
                Bloom filter false positives: 0
                Bloom filter false ratio: 0.00000
                Bloom filter space used: 16
                Compacted partition minimum bytes: 1598
                Compacted partition maximum bytes: 1916
                Compacted partition mean bytes: 1916
                Average live cells per slice (last five minutes): 2.0
                Maximum live cells per slice (last five minutes): 2.0
                Average tombstones per slice (last five minutes): 0.0
                Maximum tombstones per slice (last five minutes): 0.0
```

nodetool cfhistograms

The cfhistograms command is used to get data distribution of various metrics on a column family. The syntax for fetching histograms is as follows:

```
nodetool <connection-options> cfhistograms <keyspace-name> <column-
family-name>
```

The following is the output of running the `cfhistograms` command on the `status_updates_by_user` column family in the `apachecassandraexample` keyspace. We can see that 50 percent of read requests have a read latency of less than or equal to 535 microseconds. The minimum read latency is approximately 90 microseconds and the maximum is 634 microseconds:

```
[cassandra@apachecassandra apache-cassandra-2.1.9]$ nodetool cfhistograms apachecassandraexample status_updates_by_user
No SSTables exists, unable to calculate 'Partition Size' and 'Cell Count' percentiles
apachecassandraexample/status_updates_by_user histograms
Percentile  SSTables     Write Latency      Read Latency    Partition Size    Cell Count
                            (micros)           (micros)         (bytes)
50%           1.00           215.00             535.00            NaN            NaN
75%           1.00           215.00             535.00            NaN            NaN
95%           1.00           310.00             642.00            NaN            NaN
98%           1.00           310.00             642.00            NaN            NaN
99%           1.00           310.00             642.00            NaN            NaN
Min           0.00           125.00             180.00            NaN            NaN
Max           1.00           310.00             642.00            NaN            NaN
```

nodetool netstats

The `netstats` command shows the network-related information of a Cassandra node. It can be useful to monitor processes, such as the status of a read repair or cluster rebuild. Its syntax is:

```
Nodetool <connection-options> netstats
```

The following is a sample output of this command:

```
[cassandra@apachecassandra apache-cassandra-2.1.9]$ nodetool -h 127.0.0.1 netstats
Mode: NORMAL
Not sending any streams.
Read Repair Statistics:
Attempted: 1
Mismatch (Blocking): 0
Mismatch (Background): 0
Pool Name                    Active      Pending       Completed
Commands                      n/a           0               0
Responses                     n/a           0               0
[cassandra@apachecassandra apache-cassandra-2.1.9]$
```

nodetool tpstats

This command provides information about different Cassandra tasks such as **ReadStage** and **ReadRepairStage** using the thread pool. It is used as follows:

```
nodetool <connection-options> tpstats
```

A sample output of this command is as follows:

```
[cassandra@apachecassandra apache-cassandra-2.1.9]$ nodetool -h 127.0.0.1 tpstats
Pool Name                    Active   Pending      Completed   Blocked  All time blocked
CounterMutationStage            0         0              0         0                 0
ReadStage                       0         0             76         0                 0
RequestResponseStage            0         0              0         0                 0
MutationStage                   0         0              9         0                 0
ReadRepairStage                 0         0              0         0                 0
GossipStage                     0         0              0         0                 0
CacheCleanupExecutor            0         0              0         0                 0
AntiEntropyStage                0         0              0         0                 0
MigrationStage                  0         0              3         0                 0
Sampler                         0         0              0         0                 0
ValidationExecutor              0         0              0         0                 0
CommitLogArchiver               0         0              0         0                 0
MiscStage                       0         0              0         0                 0
MemtableFlushWriter             0         0             13         0                 0
MemtableReclaimMemory           0         0             13         0                 0
PendingRangeCalculator          0         0              1         0                 0
MemtablePostFlush               0         0             50         0                 0
CompactionExecutor              0         0            486         0                 0
InternalResponseStage           0         0              0         0                 0
HintedHandoff                   0         0              0         0                 0

Message type          Dropped
RANGE_SLICE                 0
READ_REPAIR                 0
PAGED_RANGE                 0
BINARY                      0
READ                        0
MUTATION                    0
_TRACE                      0
REQUEST_RESPONSE            0
COUNTER_MUTATION            0
[cassandra@apachecassandra apache-cassandra-2.1.9]$
```

JConsole

Other than CLI, we can monitor a Cassandra node using JConsole by connecting JConsole to its JMX port. JConsole is packaged with Java by default. The default value for the JMX port is 7199. JConsole lets us monitor our Cassandra nodes remotely. Since JConsole consumes resources heavily, we should not run JConsole on the same machine that hosts one of our Cassandra nodes.

In order to start monitoring our Cassandra server, we need to run JConsole and then select the **Remote Process** radio button. In the text box, enter the Cassandra node information in the format <Cassandra-Node>:<Cassandra-JMX-Port>. In our example, since we're running Cassandra on the local machine and using the default Cassandra JMX port, it would be **localhost:7199**. Then, enter the username and password information, which we will leave blank, since we're not using any authentication in our example. After entering this information, click on the **Connect** button, as shown in the following screenshot:

Upon successful connection, we'll have the JConsole window as shown in following figure. If the connection fails, we need to check whether the JMX port we're using is correct. The connection might also fail if our Cassandra node is running behind a firewall and JConsole cannot directly connect to it. In such a case, firewall rules might need to be updated to allow such connections.

As we can see, this window has four different tabs:

- **Overview**: This tab displays summarized details about CPU usage, memory usage, thread counts and classes loaded in a graphical view.

- **Memory**: Memory consumption, memory pool details and GC details can be monitored via this tab. In our example snapshot in the following image, we can see how Heap Memory usage varies over time. We can see that the maximum Heap memory used is ~150Mb. Also, the GC Time section in the image shows that New Generation Garbage Collection takes ~0.5 seconds and invokes 22 times; however, Old generation Garbage Collection is never invoked.

- **Threads**: This tab provides information about thread use. Here we can see the total number of threads over time. Also, this tab gives details about individual threads.

- **Classes**: Class loading details are found here.
- **VM Summary**: The Java Virtual Machine summary is provided by this tab. Here we can find details such as version, vendor, architecture, and so on.
- **MBeans**: This tab shows details about the Java MBeans registered with this MBean server. Details of these MBeans are discussed in the following section.

Let's have a look at the following figure:

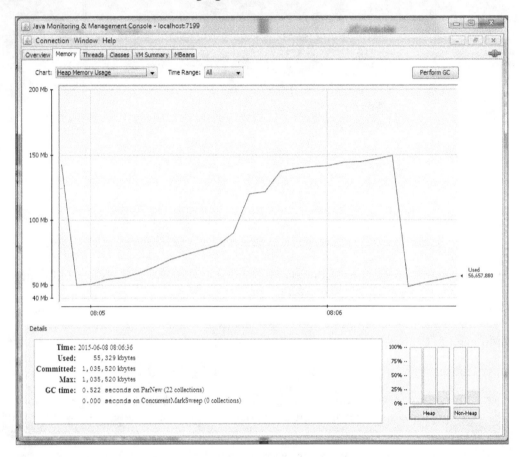

There is an **MBeans** tab, which is useful for monitoring what's going on inside our Cassandra application. There are various MBean categories available:

- `Org.apache.cassandra.db`: This contains database storage information like the total keyspaces, the partitioner being used, live node information, and cluster information.
- `Org.apache.cassandra.internal`: This contains metrics like the `GossipStage` and `HintedHandoff` state.

- Org.apache.cassandra.metrics: This is one of the most commonly used MBeans, which gives us information such as the read/write latency, cache usage, and hit rate.

- Org.apache.cassandra.net: This contains networking attributes such as MessagingService task information and FailureDetector attributes.

- Org.apache.cassandra.request: This contains the attributes of different Cassandra requests, such as ReadRequest, ReadRepairRequest, RequestResponseStage, and so on.

The following figure shows details of MBean org.apache.cassandra.metrics:typ e=ClientRequest,scope=Read,name=Latency. Here, we're observing Read Latency attributes and as we can see, the total count is 1, which means we've performed only one read operation while taking this snapshot. We can see that this read operation took around 14 microseconds. Since we've performed only one request, the values for 50thPercentile, 75thPercentile, 95thPercentile and so on are the same, that is, **13944.775** microseconds:

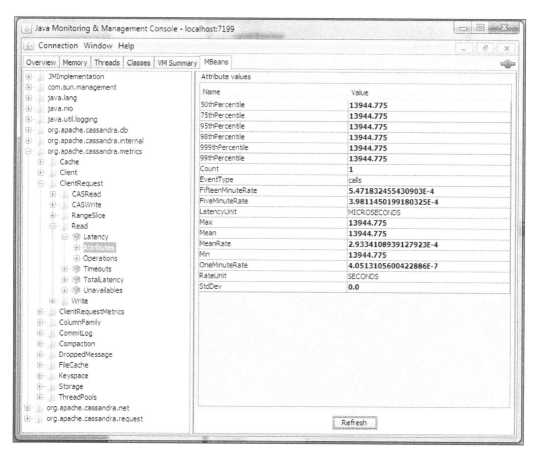

Third-party tools

The Nodetool CLI and JMX are built-in features of Apache Cassandra. There are other third-party tools that are available to monitor and manage a Cassandra cluster. A list of these tools can be found at https://wiki.apache.org/cassandra/Administration%20Tools.

Tuning Cassandra nodes

Cassandra provides various configuration options both at column family level and system level; this lets us customize Cassandra's features to suit our requirements. Let's discuss these configuration options.

Configuring Cassandra caches

From our discussion about caches in the previous chapters, we know that Cassandra has two caching options:

- **Key cache**: This caches partition keys and their respective data offset in the SSTable. When a key cache is hit, we'll save one disk seek for that SSTable search.

- **Row cache**: This stores the entire row of a partition key; in the new version, we can specify the number of rows to be stored per partition key. This caches two disk seeks as the entire row is in the memory.

Both of these caches can be configured per column family using the CQL command as we discussed in *Chapter 4, Read and Write – Behind the Scenes*.

However, there are configuration options for both of these caching types in the Cassandra.yaml file, which lets us do configurations at the system level. By default, row caching is disabled in Cassandra.yaml.

For key caching, there is a configuration option **key_cache_size_in_mb**, which defines the maximum size of the key cache in memory. By default, it is 100 MB or 5 percent of Heap in MB, whichever is less. If we want to disable key cache system wide, we should set it to 0.

For key caching, there is another configuration option called `key_cache_save_period`, which defines the number of intervals after which the cached partition key will be saved to disk at the location defined by the configuration option `saved_caches_ directory`. By default, its value is 4 hours. This option is useful while restarting a Cassandra node. After the node is restarted, the memory will be cleared and there will be no key cache; it will be populated again whenever a request is made for those keys. However, if the cached keys are saved, then Cassandra will load them into the memory after restarting the node, and requests can be processed faster.

We can also define the number of keys to be saved using the configuration option `key_cache_keys_to_save`. This option is disabled by default, which means all keys are saved to the disk after `key_cache_save_period` has elapsed.

For row caching, the `Cassandra.yaml` file has a configuration option `row_cache_ size_in_mb`; its default value is 0, which means no rows can be cached to memory. To enable row caching, we should set this configuration option to an appropriate value to suit our requirements. As we discussed previously, we should not use row caching with a column family with wide rows, as it'll put pressure on the system's memory.

Similarly to key cache, we can specify the duration of the interval after which row caches should be saved to the disk to optimize the restart process. The `row_cache_ save_period` configuration option lets us do that. However, since saving row caches can be highly I/O intensive, this option is disabled by default with a value of 0. The `row_cache_keys_to_save` is used to specify the number of rows to be saved after **row_cache_save_period** has elapsed. Its default value is 0, which means that all cached rows will be saved by default.

As discussed in *Chapter 4*, *Read and Write – Behind the Scenes*, we can use the `nodetool info` command to get the usage information of caching in a Cassandra node and adjust these settings accordingly.

Tuning Bloom filters

We know from our previous discussions that Bloom filters are used by Cassandra to filter out SSTables that definitely don't have a partition key. We also know that it can give false positives. A Bloom filter is useful for avoiding disk seeks when a row is scattered in various SSTables. Cassandra lets us configure the accuracy of a Bloom filter at the cost of memory, which means the higher the accuracy of a Bloom filter, the more memory it uses. Bloom filter accuracy can be adjusted per column family using CQL the **bloom_filter_fp_chance** option, which can have values from 0 to 1.0. Here, 0 signifies that Bloom filter accuracy will be 100 percent and 1.0 signifies 0 percent accuracy, thus disabling it. After changing Bloom filter accuracy, it is applied when compaction is trigged or when `upgradesstables` is called using the `nodetool` utility.

We can monitor the Bloom filter of a column family using the `nodetool cfstats` command. The following code snippet shows how the size of a Bloom filter is decreases when the accuracy is downgraded. Let's first set the probability of a Bloom filter giving false positives at 50 percent. We can use the `ALTER TABLE CQL` command for this purpose as shown here:

```
cqlsh:apachecassandraexample>
cqlsh:apachecassandraexample>
cqlsh:apachecassandraexample> ALTER TABLE status_updates_by_user WITH bloom_filter_fp_chance = 0.5;
cqlsh:apachecassandraexample>
```

As we've discussed above, in order to regenerate a Bloom filter we need to use either `upgradesstables` or trigger a compaction, so we're triggering a forced compaction for demo purposes:

```
# nodetool compact
Starting NodeTool
```

Now run the `cfstats` command to get the size of the Bloom filter. As we can see, the Bloom filter size is 48 bytes:

```
[cassandra@apachecassandra opt]$ nodetool cfstats apachecassandraexample.status_updates_by_user
Keyspace: apachecassandraexample
        Read Count: 11
        Read Latency: 0.4552727272727273 ms.
        Write Count: 9
        Write Latency: 0.244 ms.
        Pending Flushes: 0
                Table: status_updates_by_user
                SSTable count: 1
                Space used (live): 5141
                Space used (total): 5141
                Space used by snapshots (total): 0
                Off heap memory used (total): 49
                SSTable Compression Ratio: 0.35528596187175043
                Number of keys (estimate): 5
                Memtable cell count: 0
                Memtable data size: 0
                Memtable off heap memory used: 0
                Memtable switch count: 1
                Local read count: 11
                Local read latency: 0.456 ms
                Local write count: 9
                Local write latency: 0.245 ms
                Pending flushes: 0
                Bloom filter false positives: 0
                Bloom filter false ratio: 0.00000
                Bloom filter off heap memory used: 24
                Index summary off heap memory used: 17
                Compression metadata off heap memory used: 8
                Compacted partition minimum bytes: 104
                Compacted partition maximum bytes: 124
                Compacted partition mean bytes: 124
                Average live cells per slice (last five minutes): 1.0
                Maximum live cells per slice (last five minutes): 1.0
```

Now let's alter Bloom filter accuracy to 0 percent; that is, disable the Bloom filter using an `ALTER` statement:

```
cqlsh:apachecassandraexample>
cqlsh:apachecassandraexample>
cqlsh:apachecassandraexample> ALTER TABLE status_updates_by_user WITH bloom_filter_fp_chance = 1.0;
cqlsh:apachecassandraexample>
```

Now, run forced compaction again to alter Bloom filter size and then run the `cfstats` command to get the size of the Bloom filter. As we can see, the Bloom filter is disabled, hence the size of the Bloom filter for the table is 0 byte:

```
[cassandra@apachecassandra opt]$ nodetool compact
[cassandra@apachecassandra opt]$
[cassandra@apachecassandra opt]$ nodetool cfstats apachecassandraexample.status_updates_by_user
Keyspace: apachecassandraexample
        Read Count: 11
        Read Latency: 0.4552727272727273 ms.
        Write Count: 9
        Write Latency: 0.244 ms.
        Pending Flushes: 0
                Table: status_updates_by_user
                SSTable count: 1
                Space used (live): 5099
                Space used (total): 5099
                Space used by snapshots (total): 0
                Off heap memory used (total): 25
                SSTable Compression Ratio: 0.35528596187175043
                Number of keys (estimate): 5
                Memtable cell count: 0
                Memtable data size: 0
                Memtable off heap memory used: 0
                Memtable switch count: 1
                Local read count: 11
                Local read latency: 0.456 ms
                Local write count: 9
                Local write latency: 0.245 ms
                Pending flushes: 0
                Bloom filter false positives: 0
                Bloom filter false ratio: 0.00000

                Bloom filter off heap memory used: 0
                Index summary off heap memory used: 17
                Compression metadata off heap memory used: 8
                Compacted partition minimum bytes: 104
```

Typically, the Bloom filters are adjusted as per the compaction strategy being used. With compaction strategies with lower SSTable searches, we should tune Bloom filter accuracy to a lower setting.

For example, as we've discussed in *Chapter 4, Read and Write – Behind the Scenes*, a size-tiered compaction strategy is based on SSTable size and with this strategy, over time, the number of SSTables could grow, hence more SSTables might be scanned for a read operation. However, with a leveled compaction strategy 90 percent of the read operation would be satisfied by consulting only one SSTable. This implies that with leveled compaction we could decrease the accuracy of the Bloom filter as this strategy doesn't search more than one SSTable by design most of the time. This is the reason that the default value of tables with size-tiered compaction is 0.1 and 0.01 for tables with a leveled compaction strategy.

Bloom filter false positive statistics can be checked using the `nodetool cfstats` command. If we find many false positives for a family, then we should consider setting Bloom filter accuracy at a relatively higher value.

Configuring and tuning Java

Cassandra is heavily dependent on Java resources, so, based on our usage, we might need to tune these resources. In *Chapter 1, Getting Your Cassandra Cluster Ready*, we discussed the `cassandra-env.sh` and `cassandra-in.sh` files. These files are primarily used to configure these resources.

The `cassandra-env.sh` file houses JVM, JMX, and Heap configuration options. For configuring Heap it has two variables:

- `MAX_HEAP_SIZE`: This variable defines the total memory that will be dedicated to Java heap. While configuring this option, it is advised not to set its value at more than 8 GB, as configuring it to more than 8 GB will degrade its performance due to longer Java Garbage Collection pauses.
- `HEAP_NEWSIZE`: This variable defines space for young generation.

The default value for `MAX_HEAP_SIZE` is 4 GB and for `HEAP_NEWSIZE` is 800 MB; for most 8 core and above machines, this setting should be fine. A typical recommended value is 100 MB per physical CPU core.

Cassandra dumps Garbage Collection information into its log file `system.log`. These logs are dumped by the `GCInspector.java` class. The New Generation Garbage Collection logs are marked with `ParNew`, and the Old Generation Garbage Collection logs are marked with `ConcurrentMarkSweep` using this class. The following is a sample log snippet of these logs from the `system.log` file of a development machine:

```
INFO  [Service Thread] 2015-04-20 11:50:25,666 GCInspector.java:142
- ParNew GC in 244ms.  CMS Old Gen: 440843768 -> 507433224; Par Eden
Space: 167772160 -> 0;
```

```
INFO  [Service Thread] 2015-04-20 11:50:34,777 GCInspector.java:142
- ConcurrentMarkSweep GC in 3735ms.  CMS Old Gen: 590082672 ->
201463512; CMS Perm Gen: 33103384 -> 33103064; Par Eden Space: 3149080
-> 98095112; Par Survivor Space: 20971520 -> 20952400
INFO  [Service Thread] 2015-04-20 11:50:37,969 GCInspector.java:142
- ParNew GC in 244ms.  CMS Old Gen: 224478952 -> 290647552; Par Eden
Space: 167772160 -> 0;
INFO  [Service Thread] 2015-04-20 11:50:38,722 GCInspector.java:142
- ParNew GC in 334ms.  CMS Old Gen: 290647552 -> 396064680; Par Eden
Space: 167772160 -> 0;
INFO  [Service Thread] 2015-04-20 11:50:39,379 GCInspector.java:142
- ParNew GC in 223ms.  CMS Old Gen: 396108800 -> 451377344; Par Eden
Space: 167772160 -> 0;
INFO  [Service Thread] 2015-04-20 11:50:40,085 GCInspector.java:142
- ParNew GC in 244ms.  CMS Old Gen: 472360184 -> 537433288; Par Eden
Space: 167772160 -> 0; Par Survivor Space: 20928560 -> 20971520
INFO  [Service Thread] 2015-04-20 11:50:44,942 GCInspector.java:142
- ConcurrentMarkSweep GC in 2850ms.  CMS Old Gen: 585194096 ->
117172848; CMS Perm Gen: 33103904 -> 33103872; Par Eden Space: 50864
-> 23555168; Par Survivor Space: 20971520 -> 7625264
INFO  [Service Thread] 2015-04-20 11:50:51,575 GCInspector.java:142
- ParNew GC in 258ms.  CMS Old Gen: 296450232 -> 375950824; Par Eden
Space: 167772160 -> 0;
INFO  [Service Thread] 2015-04-20 11:50:52,306 GCInspector.java:142
- ParNew GC in 339ms.  CMS Old Gen: 375950824 -> 476767832; Par Eden
Space: 167772160 -> 0;
INFO  [Service Thread] 2015-04-20 11:50:52,984 GCInspector.java:142
- ParNew GC in 207ms.  CMS Old Gen: 476767832 -> 532644040; Par Eden
Space: 167772160 -> 0;
INFO  [Service Thread] 2015-04-20 11:50:57,595 GCInspector.java:142
- ConcurrentMarkSweep GC in 3120ms.  CMS Old Gen: 583912808 ->
139724784; Code Cache: 9336192 -> 9338368; Par Eden Space: 7222568 ->
26675272; Par Survivor Space: 19073920 -> 6913040
```

In the preceding snippet, we can see New Generation Garbage collection takes approximately 200 milliseconds and the Old Generation takes approximately 3 seconds.

If all is running fine, then GC should typically take a few hundred milliseconds on the production machines. However, if it takes a long time, then there might be the need to tune the Heap space. Typically, ParNew takes longer when the rate of the New Generation is higher and its space fills faster. The ConcurrentMarkSweep collector will take longer if the Old Generation gets full; hence, it triggers to full GC. Ee might be in need of Heap size tuning in such cases.

Summary

Cassandra servers prior to version 2.1 used Log4j for logging purposes; however, from version 2.1 onwards, they use the Logback library. Cassandra logs its various activities in the `system.log` file. Logging configuration can be adjusted as per our requirements using the `log4j-server.properties` or `logback.xml` file based on the Cassandra server version you're using. The `nodetool cfstats` command provides statistics of a column family, such as memtable uses, SSTable count, and Bloom filter usage. Read/write latencies for a column family can be tracked using the `nodetool cfhistogram` utility. The `cfhistograms` command gives distribution data about latencies, partition sizes, and SSTable count. Bloom filter accuracy can be adjusted to suit our requirements. A Bloom filter with 100 percent accuracy will occupy the largest memory size. We can disable the Bloom filter by setting the configuration option **bloom_filter_fp_change** to `1.0`. The `GCInspector` class dumps Garbage Collection information into the `system.log` file. The new generation collection information logs are tagged using `ParNew` and the old generation collection information logs are tagged using `ConcurrentMarkSweep`. Typically, in a healthy node, Garbage Collection should complete in few hundred milliseconds.

7
Backup and Restore

Cassandra is a highly available peer-to-peer distributed database. Data is partitioned and replicated among multiple nodes and different data centers in Cassandra, and therefore, data backup and restore might seem redundant. However, there may be scenarios where a client application, or due to some other reason, data is corrupted and a need to recover arises. Cassandra provides recovery options and tools to take data backup. In this chapter, we'll discuss those tools and techniques. Sometimes, there may be a need to migrate data from a NoSQL database to Cassandra, so we'll discuss that too. In later parts of this chapter, we'll discuss how to replace, move, and remove nodes from a Cassandra cluster.

Taking backup of a Casandra cluster

Cassandra takes backup of data in the form of snapshots of `SSTables`. While a node is online, we can take snapshots of data stored in data files of the Cassandra data directory. While taking snapshots, we can specify whether we want to take a snapshot of all data/keyspaces, a specific keyspace, or a specific column family. These snapshots can then be moved to another location for backup, or we can leave them at the default location. Snapshots are taken node wide, and all data is contained in the snapshot that is written before a snapshot is triggered. A node's snapshot may not be consistent with another replica node. However, when snapshots of all nodes are restored, data eventually becomes consistent.

Once we have taken snapshot of all nodes, we can configure Cassandra to take incremental snapshots. Incremental backup will start an automatic snapshot trigger whenever an SSTable is flushed.

 A snapshot comprises only the data of the column family and doesn't include the schema. Also, snapshots can be restored only when the schema of the respective data exists, so it's recommended that you also back up the schema separately.

Manual backup

A snapshot is taken for each node the using nodetool snapshot command. In order to take a snapshot of the complete cluster, you'll need to run this command on each node in the cluster. While taking a snapshot, ensure that there is sufficient disk space for the new snapshots.

A manual snapshot of all keyspaces of a node can be taken as follows:

```
$ nodetool snapshot
Requested creating snapshot(s) for [all keyspaces] with snapshot name [1437860306074]
Snapshot directory: 1437860306074
$
```

Now, you can find the snapshots of all keyspaces with the following code snippet:

<data-directory>/<key-space-name>/<column-family-name-(some-random-hex-number)>/snapshots/<snapshot-name>

For example, if our data directory is /opt/Cassandra/data, the keyspace name is apache_cassandra_demo_db, the table name is user_table, and the snapshot name is 1437860306074, then the snapshot will be stored from the preceding command in the following directory:

```
/opt/Cassandra/data/apache_cassandra_demo_db/user_table-f99a8ec0110611
e5833fa9b7a6da1962/snapshots/1437860306074
```

Similarly, a snapshot of a specific keyspace or a column family can be taken as follows:

```
$ nodetool snapshot apache_cassandra_demo_db
Requested creating snapshot(s) for [apache_cassandra_demo_db] with
snapshot name [1437860924428]
Snapshot directory: 1437860924428
// snapshot of a specific column family
$nodetool snapshot -cf user_table apache_cassandra_demo_db
```

```
Requested creating snapshot(s) for [apache_cassandra_demo_db ] with
snapshot name [1437861147928]

Snapshot directory: 1437861147928

// snapshot of a specific column family with custom snapshot tag

$ nodetool snapshot -cf user_table -t user_table_snapshot apache_
cassandra_demo_db

Requested creating snapshot(s) for [apache_cassandra_demo_db ] with
snapshot name [user_table_snapshot]

Snapshot directory: user_table_snapshot
```

Deleting snapshots

When we trigger a snapshot, it doesn't delete old snapshots, if any, so we need to delete them separately. The `nodetool clearsnapshot` command helps us to delete old snapshots that are not required anymore from a Cassandra node. This command removes the snapshot with the given name from the given keyspace. We can also remove all snapshots using a single command by omitting the name of the keyspace and snapshot:

```
// Delete all snapshots from the node

$ nodetool clearsnapshot

Requested clearing snapshot(s) for [all keyspaces]

// Delete snapshot with tag name user_table_snapshot

$ nodetool clearsnapshot -t user_table_snapshot

Requested clearing snapshot(s) for [all keyspaces] with snapshot name
[user_table_snapshot]
```

Incremental backup

Incremental backup creates snapshots for each new flushed `SSTable` to back up the directory automatically, thus allowing us to have an up-to-date data backup of Cassandra. By default, this feature is disabled in Cassandra. In order to enable this feature, you'll have to set the configuration option `incremental_backups` to `true` in the `Cassandra.yaml` configuration file for each node of the cluster.

 Cassandra does not delete old backup files created by incremental backup, so, we should remove these files at regular intervals manually or via some custom automated process; for example; a script to remove these files.

Restoring data to Cassandra

In order to restore data from a snapshot onto a node, follow these steps:

1. Shut down the node.

2. Delete the old `commitlog` files:

    ```
    // package based installation
    $ rm /var/lib/cassandra/commitlog/*
    // Tar based installation
    $ rm <install-directory/data/commitlog/*
    ```

3. Delete the old `SSTable` files from `<data-dir>/<keyspace-name>/<column-family-name>/`:

    ```
    // package based installation
    $ rm /var/lib/Cassandra/data/apache_cassandra_demo_db/user_table-
    f99a8ec0110611e5833fa9b7a6da1962/*.db
    ```

    ```
    // Tar based installation, considering tar is unpacked at /opt/
    cassandra location
    $ rm /opt/cassandra/data/data/apache_cassandra_demo_db/user_table-
    f99a8ec0110611e5833fa9b7a6da1962/*.db
    ```

4. Copy the latest snapshots from the snapshot location to the data directory:

    ```
    // package based installation
    $ cp -p /var/lib/Cassandra/data/apache_cassandra_demo_db/user_
    table-f99a8ec0110611e5833fa9b7a6da1962/snapshots/1437860306074/* /
    var/lib/Cassandra/data/apache_cassandra_demo_db/user_table-f99a8ec
    0110611e5833fa9b7a6da1962/
    ```

    ```
    // Tar based installation
    $ cp -p /opt/cassandra/data/apache_cassandra_demo_db/user_table-
    f99a8ec0110611e5833fa9b7a6da1962/snapshots/1437860306074/* /opt/
    cassandra/data/apache_cassandra_demo_db/user_table-f99a8ec0110611e
    5833fa9b7a6da1962/
    ```

5. Restart the node.

6. Run the `nodetool repair` command.

 This method should be used to restore data on the nodes of the cluster on which the snapshots was taken. If data need to restore on a different node of a different cluster, then use the `sstableloader` command, as described in the next section.

The Cassandra bulk loader

Cassandra provides a command line utility called `sstableloader`. This utility is able to bulk load `SSTables` to nodes irrespective of whether they are in the same cluster or not. It contacts one of the cluster nodes to ascertain cluster information, and then copies relevant data to the nodes, unlike copying `SSTable` snapshots to the data directory as done in the previous method.

In order to use the `sstableloader` command, you need to perform the following steps:

1. Create the keyspace and tables with which data needs to be restored if they do? not exist.

2. Create a directory structure in the format `<keyspace-name>/<column-family-name>`. For example, to restore a snapshot of the keyspace `apache_cassandra_demo_db` and the column family `user_table`, create a folder as follows:

    ```
    $ mkdir -p apache_cassandra_demo_db/user_table
    ```

3. Copy the snapshot files into this directory:

    ```
    $ cp -p /opt/cassandra/data/apache_cassandra_demo_db/user_table-
    f99a8ec0110611e5833fa9b7a6da1962/snapshots/1437860306074/* /opt/
    backup/apache_cassandra_demo_db/user_table
    ```

4. Run the `sstableloader` command, giving the address of one of the nodes of the cluster in which you need to load the data:

    ```
    $ sstableloader -d 10.78.175.22 /opt/backup/apache_cassandra_demo_
    db/user_table
    ```

    Established connection to initial hosts

    Opening sstables and calculating sections to stream

    Streaming relevant part of /opt/backup/apache_cassandra_demo_db/
    user_table/apache_cassandra_demo_db-user_table-ka-3-Data.db to
    [/10.78.175.17, /10.78.175.23, /10.78.175.122, /10.78.175.22,
    /10.78.175.92]

    progress: [/10.78.175.22]0:1/1 100% [/10.78.175.92]0:1/1 100%
    total: 100% 0 MB/s(avg: 0 MB/s)

    Summary statistics:

Connections per host:	: 1
Total files transferred:	: 2
Total bytes transferred:	: 164
Total duration (ms):	: 2690
Average transfer rate (MB/s):	: 0
Peak transfer rate (MB/s):	: 0

Exporting and importing data using the Cassandra JSON utility

Other than taking snapshots, it's also possible to export column family data from SSTables to JSON format and then convert that JSON data into a SSTable, which can then be loaded into Cassandra.

The Cassandra utility command sstabl2json is used to convert SSTables to JSON format. The output of this utility is sent to STDOUT, so we need to redirect it to some file if needed. Follow the given steps to export a SSTable to JSON format:

1. Identify the path of the SSTable data file that you want to convert on a node. SSTable data files end with –Data.db.

2. Use the sstable2json command to convert a copy of it into the JSON format:

   ```
   $ sstable2json /opt/cassandra/dsc-cassandra-2.1.2/data/data/
   apache_cassandra_db/user_table-fd3522d0e27011e4a51b811a5d39e8fc/
   apache_cassandra_db-user_table-ka-3-Data.db > /backups/user_table_
   backup.json
   ```

3. This JSON file can then be backed up and later converted to an SSTable and loaded into Cassandra, as follows:

   ```
   $ json2sstable -K apache_cassandra_db -c user_table /backups/user_
   table_backup.json  apache_cassandra_db-user_table-ka-3-Data.db
   ```

Loading external data into Cassandra

Sometimes, we might need to have some data from another database system, and we may want that data to be loaded to our Cassandra cluster. For example, we might have data containing CSV that needs to be uploaded. In such scenarios, we can use the Cassandra Java library class CQLSSTableWriter to convert the data into a SSTable and then generate a SSTable that can be loaded to Cassandra using the sstableloader utility.

Suppose that we have a CSV file input.csv, with data like the following code:

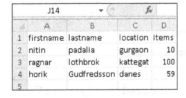

The Cassandra schema in to which we want to load this data is as follows:

```
CREATE TABLE apache_cassandra_db.user_table (
```

```
        firstname text,
        lastname text,
        location text,
        items int,
        PRIMARY KEY ((firstname, lastname), location)
)
```

To do this, we first create a `CQLSSTableWriter` instance mapped with our schema, and an `Insert` statement specifying how to insert data into our column family as follows:

```
String SCHEMA = String.format("CREATE TABLE %s.%s (" +
                                "firstname text, " +
                                "lastname text, " +
                                "location text, " +
                                "items int, " +
                                "PRIMARY KEY ((firstname,
lastname), location)" +
                                ") ", KEYSPACE, TABLE);


// Insert Statement
String INSERT_STMT = String.format("INSERT INTO %s.%s (" +
                                "firstname, lastname, location, items" +
                                ") VALUES (" +
                                "?, ?, ?, ?" +
                                ")", KEYSPACE, TABLE);
// Writer Instance
CQLSSTableWriter.Builder builder = CQLSSTableWriter.builder();

builder.inDirectory(outputDir)
            .forTable(SCHEMA)
            .using(INSERT_STMT)

            .withPartitioner(new Murmur3Partitioner());
```

Once a `writer` instance is created, read rows from the CSV and add it to the writer, as follows. Finally, close the writer:

```
List<String> lineReadFromCSV;
while ((lineReadFromCSV = csvReader.read()) != null)
{
    writer.addRow(new String(lineReadFromCSV.get(0)),
                new String(lineReadFromCSV.get(1)),
                new String(lineReadFromCSV.get(2)),
                Integer.parseInt(lineReadFromCSV.get(3))
                );
}
```

Note that while adding a row, each column read from the CSV is mapped to its respective data type supported by Cassandra. For example, the text is mapped to a string, and int is mapped to an integer. Data type mapping can be found at http://docs.datastax.com/en/developer/java-driver/2.0/java-driver/reference/javaClass2Cql3Datatypes_r.html.

The complete program is listed as follows:

```java
package apache.cassandra.essentials;

import java.io.BufferedReader;
import java.io.File;
import java.io.FileReader;
import java.io.IOException;

import org.apache.cassandra.config.Config;
import org.apache.cassandra.exceptions.InvalidRequestException;
import org.apache.cassandra.io.sstable.CQLSSTableWriter;

public class CSVToSSTable {

  public static final String CSV_FILE = "resources/input.csv";

  public static final String SSTABLE_OUTPUT_DIR = "./sstable";

  public static final String KEYSPACE = "apache_cassandra_db";

  public static final String TABLE = "user_table";

  public static final String CSV_DELIMITER = ",";

  public static final String TABLE_SCHEMA = String.format("CREATE
TABLE %s.%s ("
      + "firstname text, " + "lastname text, " + "location text, "
      + "items int, " + "PRIMARY KEY ((firstname, lastname),
location)"
      + ") ", KEYSPACE, TABLE);

  public static final String INSERT_STMT = String.format(
      "INSERT INTO %s.%s (" + "firstname, lastname, location, items"
        + ") VALUES (" + "?, ?, ?, ?" + ")", KEYSPACE, TABLE);
```

```
public static void main(String[] args) {

    // create SSTable inside <keyspace-name>/<table-name> folder as
same is
    // supported by Cassandra sstableloader command line utility
    File outputDir = new File(SSTABLE_OUTPUT_DIR + File.separator
        + KEYSPACE + File.separator + TABLE);
    if (!outputDir.exists() && !outputDir.mkdirs()) {
      throw new RuntimeException("Unable to create directory: "
          + outputDir);
    }

    // Tell library that we're running in client mode and don't have
    // cassandra.yaml
    Config.setClientMode(true);

    // Get SSTable writer builder
    CQLSSTableWriter.Builder builder = CQLSSTableWriter.builder();

    // configure builder and get a writer
    CQLSSTableWriter writer = builder.inDirectory(outputDir) // set
output
                                    // directory
        .forTable(TABLE_SCHEMA) // set column family mapping
        .using(INSERT_STMT) // set Insert statement mapping
        .build();

    try (BufferedReader reader = new BufferedReader(
        new FileReader(CSV_FILE))) {

      // skip header
      String line = reader.readLine();

      String[] row = null;

      // Read rows from CSV File and add to writer
      while ((line = reader.readLine()) != null) {
        row = line.split(CSV_DELIMITER);
        writer.addRow(new String(row[0]),
            new String(row[1]),
            new String(row[2]),
            Integer.parseInt(row[3]));
      }
```

```
        // Flush SSTable write
        writer.close();
    } catch (InvalidRequestException | IOException e) {
        e.printStackTrace();
    }


    }
}
```

When we run this program, it creates a `SSTable` in the folder hierarchy `sstable/apache_cassandra_db/user_table`, as shown in the following screenshot:

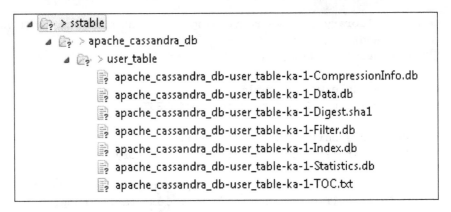

After that, run the `sstableloader` command to load this data into Cassandra:

```
$ cd sstables
$ sstableloader -d 10.78.171.183 apache_cassandra_db/user_table/
Established connection to initial hosts
Opening sstables and calculating sections to stream
Streaming relevant part of apache_cassandra_db/user_table/apache_
cassandra_db-user_table-ka-1-Data.db to [/10.76.214.57, /10.76.214.243,
/10.76.214.242, /10.78.171.183, /10.76.214.102]
progress: [/10.76.214.57]0:1/1 100% [/10.76.214.243]0:1/1
100% [/10.76.214.242]0:1/1 100% [/10.78.171.183]0:1/1 100%
[/10.76.214.102]0:1/1 100% total: 100% 0   MB/s(avg: 0 MB/s)
Summary statistics:
    Connections per host:        : 1
    Total files transferred:     : 5
    Total bytes transferred:     : 990
    Total duration (ms):         : 2560
    Average transfer rate (MB/s): : 0
    Peak transfer rate (MB/s):   : 0
```

Removing nodes from Cassandra cluster

Sometimes, we might need to reduce the size of a cluster due to a dead node or a machine with old hardware. In such scenarios, the remaining nodes must take responsibility for the data ranges of the dead node or the node that is being removed. Cassandra provides a command-line utility for both scenarios.

If a node is down and we want to remove it from the cluster, then we should run `nodetool removenode <Dead-Node-ID>` from some other node. This command streams the data for which this node was responsible to remaining nodes from the remaining replicas. In order to get the dead node `ID`, we can use the `nodetool status` command, as follows:

```
$ nodetool status

Datacenter: datacenter1

========================

Status=Up/Down

|/ State=Normal/Leaving/Joining/Moving

--  Address          Load       Tokens  Owns     Host ID
Rack
DN  10.76.215.17  225.04 MB  256     ?        940ba0cf-b75a-448c-a15e-
40e05efbeb34   rack1

UN  10.76.215.24  191.04 MB  256     ?        4b728c3c-c545-4e4d-b1aa-
62f66ef6bdce   rack1

UN  10.76.215.42  230.83 MB  256     ?        d63a18c4-0d2c-4574-8f66-
c4eb1e5ca5a8   rack1

UN  10.76.215.18  235.75 MB  256     ?        2f9bb0a9-db48-4146-83c6-
4ce06bd22259   rack1

UN  10.76.215.10  222.21 MB  256     ?        1ffe9ddb-9e3e-4060-8da2-
3cc6d3171d3a   rack1
```

Note that our first node is down with the host ID `940ba0cf-b75a-448c-a15e-40e05efbeb34`. Therefore, we will run the `removenode` command, as follows, to remove this node from cluster. Use the `nodetool removenode status` command to check the progress of this process later on:

```
$ nodetool removenode 940ba0cf-b75a-448c-a15e-40e05efbeb34

// Check if remove node complete

$ nodetool removenode status

RemovalStatus: No token removals in process.

// Process complete now node should be removed from nodetool status
output
```

```
$ nodetool status

Datacenter: datacenter1

========================

Status=Up/Down

|/ State=Normal/Leaving/Joining/Moving
```

--	Address	Load	Tokens	Owns	Host ID
Rack					
UN	10.76.215.24	191.04 MB	256	?	4b728c3c-c545-4e4d-b1aa-
62f66ef6bdce	rack1				
UN	10.76.215.42	230.83 MB	256	?	d63a18c4-0d2c-4574-8f66-
c4eb1e5ca5a8	rack1				
UN	10.76.215.18	235.75 MB	256	?	2f9bb0a9-db48-4146-83c6-
4ce06bd22259	rack1				
UN	10.76.215.10	222.21 MB	256	?	1ffe9ddb-9e3e-4060-8da2-
3cc6d3171d3a	rack1				

 [If your cluster doesn't use vnodes, then you should consider adjusting, token distribution among nodes in order to balance data distribution among them.]

If a node is not down and we want to decommission it, then we use the `nodetool decommission` command to assign the data ranges that this node was responsible for to the remaining nodes in the cluster. This command can be run on the node that is being removed. The following is the cluster status after decommissioning one node:

```
$ nodetool status

Datacenter: datacenter1

========================

Status=Up/Down

|/ State=Normal/Leaving/Joining/Moving
```

--	Address	Load	Tokens	Owns	Host ID
Rack					
UN	10.76.215.24	191.04 MB	256	?	4b728c3c-c545-4e4d-b1aa-
62f66ef6bdce	rack1				
UN	10.76.215.42	230.83 MB	256	?	d63a18c4-0d2c-4574-8f66-
c4eb1e5ca5a8	rack1				
UN	10.76.215.18	235.75 MB	256	?	2f9bb0a9-db48-4146-83c6-
4ce06bd22259	rack1				

Data doesn't get removed from the node being decommissioned; hence, if we are adding a decommissioned node to some other cluster range, we should remove the data manually.

Adding nodes to a Cassandra cluster

In order to add a node to a Cassandra cluster, you should consider the following configuration options in the Cassandra.yaml file:

- auto_bootstrap: Set this configuration option to true so that a newly joining node can collect data from other nodes.

- listen_address: Set this to the appropriate IP address of the node.

- endpoint_snitch: Ensure that the new node is using the same snitch as that being used by the other nodes.

- seed_provider: This lists the nodes that are in the seed node list in the existing cluster. Since this new node is bootstrapping, it can't be in the seed node list right now.

- cluster_name: Ensure that the cluster name is the same as that of the other nodes in the cluster.

In the Cassandra-rackdc.properties file, update the correct datacentre and rack information for the new node. After ensuring that all configurations are good, start Cassandra on this new node. Once the new node is up and running, execute the nodetool cleanup command on all nodes other than this new node to clean up the partition keys that those nodes are no longer handling.

Replacing dead nodes in a cluster

To replace a dead node, we should first remove that node using the nodetool removenode command as described earlier, and then we should add the new node as discussed in the previous section.

 If the new node's IP address is different to the previous dead node's IP address, then start Cassandra on the new node with the startup parameter replace_address=<IP-address-of-dead-node>.

To replace a node that is alive and being replaced due to hardware upgrade or another such reason, we should first add the new node and then decommission the old node using the nodetool decommission command, as discussed previously.

Summary

Cassandra is a highly available, fault-tolerant, distributed database. However, sometimes data can get corrupted due to client application faults and other reasons. To handle such situations, Cassandra provides tools to back up and restore data to the last known state. Using the `nodetool snapshot` command, we can manually take snapshots of the data of a node. Restoring the snapshot from a node might not be consistents but restoring from all nodes' data will eventually become consistent. An incremental backup configuration allows the taking of automatic snapshots of node data. While loading `SSTables` in the bulk `sstableloader` is a great utility, using the `sstableloader` `SSTables` can be uploaded to different clusters with different ranges and replication factors too. The `sstable2json` command converts a `SSTable` to JSON format, which then can be converted back to `SSTable` using the `json2sstable` command and be loaded into a Cassandra node. The `CQLSSTableWriter` class APIs can be used to create the `SSTable` from external data, such as a CSV file. Cassandra provides command line utilities to add, remove, or replace Cassandra nodes.

Index

A

architecture, Cassandra 15, 16

B

backup
  about 133
  incremental backup 135
  manual backup 134
batch statements 58, 107
Bigtable 15
Bloom filters
  tuning 127-129

C

Cassandra bulk loader
  about 137
  external data, loading 138-142
Cassandra caches
  configuring 126, 127
  Key cache 126
  Row cache 126
Cassandra cluster
  compiling, from source 3
  connecting to 87-89
  failure detection 22
  Gossip protocol 17-21
  installation 1, 3
  installing, from precompiled binary 4
  logs, used for debugging 118
  monitoring 117
  monitoring, command line utilities
      used 118

monitoring, JConsole used 122-125
monitoring, third-party tools used 126
nodes, adding 30-32
overview 16, 17
policies 90
prerequisites 2, 3
reading/writing 93, 94
reading/writing, asynchronously 96, 97
reading/writing, with batch statements 107
reading/writing, with prepared
      statement 101-105
reading/writing, with QueryBuilder 95
Cassandra JSON utility
  used, for exporting data 138
  used, for importing data 138
Cassandra queries
  tracing 84, 85
  tracing, Java driver used 114, 115
Cassandra server
  Cassandra node, running 10
  cluster, setting up 11, 12
  cluster status, viewing 12
  running 10
Cassandra.yaml file, configuration options
  auto_bootstrap 145
  cluster_name 145
  endpoint_snitch 145
  listen_address 145
  seed_provider 145
cfhistograms command 120
cfstats command
  about 119
  using 119, 120
client drivers
  reference link 87

H

hinted handoff
about 81
consistency levels, for write
operation 81-83

I

incremental backup 135
installation layout
about 5
package-based installation 6
tarball installations 5

J

Java
configuring 130, 131
tuning 130, 131
JConsole
Classes tab 124
MBeans tab 124
Memory tab 123
Overview tab 123
Threads tab 123
used, for monitoring Cassandra
cluster 122-125
VM Summary tab 124

K

keyspace
about 35, 36
creating 32

L

leveled compaction 70, 71
Lightweight Transaction (LWT) 57-80
list 47, 48
load balancing policies 91, 92

M

manual backup
about 134
snapshots, deleting 135

map 48
mapping API
about 108
example 108-110
implementing 110-112
Memtable 64
multiple clustering columns 42

N

netstats command 121
NetworkTopologyStrategy
about 26
snitches 27, 28
nodes
adding 145
adding, to cluster 30-32
Bloom filters, tuning 127-129
Cassandra caches, configuring 126, 127
Java, configuring 130, 131
Java, tuning 130, 131
removing 143, 144
replacing 145
tuning 126
nodetool repair 36
nodetool utility
about 117, 118
cfhistograms command 120
cfstats command 119, 120
netstats command 121
tpstats command 121

P

package-based installation
directory layout 6
partition key
about 15, 37
conditional querying 54, 55
phi accrual failure detector
reference link 22
policies, Cassandra cluster
about 90
load balancing policies 91, 92
reconnection policies 92
retry policies 92
prepared statement 101-105

Thank you for buying
Apache Cassandra Essentials

About Packt Publishing

Packt, pronounced 'packed', published its first book, *Mastering phpMyAdmin for Effective MySQL Management*, in April 2004, and subsequently continued to specialize in publishing highly focused books on specific technologies and solutions.

Our books and publications share the experiences of your fellow IT professionals in adapting and customizing today's systems, applications, and frameworks. Our solution-based books give you the knowledge and power to customize the software and technologies you're using to get the job done. Packt books are more specific and less general than the IT books you have seen in the past. Our unique business model allows us to bring you more focused information, giving you more of what you need to know, and less of what you don't.

Packt is a modern yet unique publishing company that focuses on producing quality, cutting-edge books for communities of developers, administrators, and newbies alike. For more information, please visit our website at www.packtpub.com.

About Packt Open Source

In 2010, Packt launched two new brands, Packt Open Source and Packt Enterprise, in order to continue its focus on specialization. This book is part of the Packt Open Source brand, home to books published on software built around open source licenses, and offering information to anybody from advanced developers to budding web designers. The Open Source brand also runs Packt's Open Source Royalty Scheme, by which Packt gives a royalty to each open source project about whose software a book is sold.

Writing for Packt

We welcome all inquiries from people who are interested in authoring. Book proposals should be sent to author@packtpub.com. If your book idea is still at an early stage and you would like to discuss it first before writing a formal book proposal, then please contact us; one of our commissioning editors will get in touch with you.

We're not just looking for published authors; if you have strong technical skills but no writing experience, our experienced editors can help you develop a writing career, or simply get some additional reward for your expertise.